I0167678

Also by Tony Brennan

The Bexford North Mysteries:

1. *And The Dance Goes On*

2. *The Black Lamb*

3. *The Blight of Lady Emily*

4. *The Bell Tolled Twice*

5. *Death and the Lazy Milkmaid*

6. *Death and the Dowagers*

*

A Healthy Death

*

Short Stories

Is there Anyone There?

*

Trilogy

Eminently Respectable Capers

Gertrude

Jumpin' Jerusalem! He's Back!

JUMPIN' JERUSALEM... HE'S BACK!

If ever I did see, a dead man it was He!

(THE LAST BOOK IN THE TRILOGY)

TONY BRENNAN

Copyright © 2019 Tony Brennan

ISBN: 978-1-925952-66-7
Published by Vivid Publishing
P.O. Box 948, Fremantle
Western Australia 6959
www.vividpublishing.com.au

Cataloguing-in-Publication data is available from the National Library of Australia

All rights reserved. No part of this book may be reproduced in any form whatsoever.

This is a work of fiction. Any resemblance to any person living or dead is entirely coincidental. In depicting people holding public office, no offence or ridicule is intended whatsoever. The British Prime Minister and the monarch and her consort are accorded great respect. Any flippancy is not intended to be derisory, simply amusing. The 'Northern Historic Park' in Australia is a product of the author's imagination. Nothing in the description is based on any similar historic village in Australia, or elsewhere, to the author's knowledge. However, the Battle of Vinegar Hill is an historic fact in the history of early Australia; the re-enactment of the battle is solely imagined by the author.

"...God deliver me from sour saints!"

Teresa of Avila.

Saint, Mystic and Doctor of the Church

WHAT'S IN A NAME?

"Has he spoken yet?"

"Well, he's mumbled a bit, Doctor," answered the nurse. "It doesn't make much sense. Whenever I ask him his name, he mutters something like…'Harl', or I suppose it could be, 'Karl'… that's all. Sounds foreign to me."

The Doctor was studying the patient closely. He looked up at the nurse.

"Could it be 'Charles', by any chance, Nurse? He looks English to me, or…I suppose it's possible… but, he could even be American."

The Head Nurse was examining the thin, emaciated body of the elderly man. "There's something strange about this one, Doctor. He's been through a tough time, his body bears witness to that… but, there's something different about him – he's not a deadbeat, like our usual ones; I think he's been someone important; he has beautiful hands.

"Even though – as I said – he mumbles, he occasionally says whole words and he has a beautiful voce. *Cultured*, I mean. This is a highly educated man, I'll wager."

"Well, keep me informed on this one, Nurse. We'll call him 'Charles', just for the time being. All his tests show no alcohol, no diseases at all, blood pressure is low but that would be expected in his case – whatever happened to make him a '*case*' – but the temperature is rapidly approaching normal since we got the tubes into him."

"Doctor, I was wondering what all those smallish, holes were in his legs and feet. I know it sounds ridiculous, but it looks as if some creatures were eating him."

The doctor smiled, genuinely amused. "Nurse, I think you're 'spot-on'. When I first examined him, I was told he'd been rescued at sea. I immediately thought of either, crabs, or small fish. I think I could be right. The salt-water would have prevented them from becoming infectious." He laughed quietly. "Well, if he ever wakes up, and is 'cognitively intact', we might actually *know*."

The doctor moved away. "Let me know, at once, Nurse, if there is any change. I want this one to live; I think he has many more years to live, if we can waken him properly; he is a healthy man – old – of course – but a very *healthy*, old man."

The nurse nodded as the doctor moved on down the ward. She then spoke softly to the man in the bed. "Listen, Charles, I'm going to give you a good sleep; you've had all you can hold through the tubes, but a good sleep to warm you up might do the trick. I'll see you when you wake up." She flipped a switch, and after checking all the monitors, gently pulled the curtains around the bed.

The Head Nurse then resumed her work, with the other patients, in the Intensive Care ward.

THE EMPTY COFFIN REQUIEM

Back in Australia, the Archbishop of the city, the very Reverend Samuel Spotels, helped the limping nun down the Cathedral steps, when the solemn requiem he had recently offered was finished for the beloved, and mischievous, old Cardinal, Charles York.

As the body had never been recovered it was a Requiem with an open coffin. The cathedral was packed and was over-flowing with flowers.

Mother Angelica had fallen again in the devastation that had resulted in the sudden flooding of their Retirement Home. The fall had exacerbated a previous injury. That injury had first occurred when the old cardinal had accidentally blown up the Sisters' previous city Home, on Guy Fawkes' night.

The Archbishop was concerned for the good Mother Superior of the little group of Sisters who staffed the Home. Mother Angelica seemed to have aged a great deal in the months since the floods – she was glad of the steady arm of the young Archbishop.

The two friends stood talking near their small bus, with Sister Maria patiently waiting in the driver's seat. Sister Margaret and the oldest members of her community, Sister Veronica and Sister Bernard, were already waiting inside the bus.

"Your Grace," Angelica looked up at the tall prelate. "Have

you been able to come to grips with the death of the old one, yet? I ask that, as I simply cannot believe he's gone. I have the strongest feeling we're missing something; that he'll turn up, as he's always done, and be genuinely surprised when he hears of the devastation he has caused."

The Archbishop laughed quietly. "To be utterly frank, I think as you do, Mother, but we *must* be wrong. It's months now and he would have turned up *somewhere*, by now, if he was going to turn up, at all." He sighed.

"I had postponed the Requiem for as long as I dared. Even during the long and beautiful solemn pontifical Requiem for Charles, I kept expecting him to be seen, at any moment, watching on from the choir stalls, checking that I'm doing it all correctly." He smiled sadly.

"No, Mother, I'm not over it and I don't expect I'll ever be, completely. He was such a vital part of my life; it all seems, somehow empty, without him. Even though, as you know, so very well, he gave us every grey hair we have." He laughed. "And, he caused us untold anxiety with all his tricks, surprises and his 'plans' to fix everything."

Angelica smiled; her eyes misty. "You and I think the same, Your Grace. All through the Requiem I kept expecting a leg to appear over the side of the empty coffin on the catafalque, and out would pop the old villain with one of his improbable stories…"

"…and with his excuses which always began: 'I didn't really intend…'" added Sammy.

They both laughed. Sammy became serious. "Mother, a quick word about your property. What's the situation now? Are you liable for the costs of the whole debacle? That would run into millions and millions.

"We, that is the Archdiocese, could certainly share the expenses as our old priests were there in your Home – and actually *caused* the catastrophe - but, there'd be a limit as to how *much* we could pay; I expect the same goes for your Congregation…?"

"Exactly so, Your Grace," replied Angelica. "We are not a large and wealthy Congregation, but of course, we are insured for just about everything. However, the lawyers are still in a huddle trying to discover just *what* we were responsible for, and for how much… and for what we are *not*."

"It was the shops that were worrying me, Mother. I mean they were virtually destroyed, weren't they? Everything would've had to be replaced; then would come the loss of income caused by the damage, and the repairs which took several weeks to be completed, I understand." The Archbishop closed his eyes.

"Then on top of all that, what about the attitude of all the local people – not just the shopkeepers – towards you and your charges, now? I had mental visions of you being banned from the local shops, and even the whole community of St Francis' Home being stoned, if you appeared in the streets of the town."

Angelica laughed again, and this time for a moment, revealing the happy woman she had been before the disaster happened. She shook her fingers at the Archbishop. "Now, then, you sound just like the old cardinal. I think you might have begun to think as he did.

"To answer your question: no, the local people have been simply wonderful and so kind – so unbelievably kind – after what we had done to them. They even brought food to the Home during the first dreadful days when we couldn't use the roads; they came by boat, bringing loads of food. Thank God they did; I had no idea how we were to even get out to buy the food.

"When the army, using bulldozers put the bank of the river back where it should have been and the river was flowing back into our own dam, the army also helped us in digging trenches to get the water away, which enabled us to save nearly all the cows, and hens as well."

"Thank God for that! What about the two monks? Are they still there? Were they injured at all, and what about their beloved birds? I know how much they loved those birds..."

"Definitely, Brother Joseph of Cupertino and Brother Isidore the Farmer, are still there; they were invaluable in directing the soldiers in their work in the fields and, now that the soil has dried out, they have sowed another crop in 'Sister Maria's paddock', as we call it. She ploughed it all again. The monks planted the seed for another crop of Lucerne Hay which will be used now for the cows – it was going to be for our dearest Gertrude," Angelica sniffed. "Anyhow, it will be in remembrance of her.

"As for the birds. No worry, Your Grace. When the catastrophe occurred, the brothers rushed out into the rising waters – water, literally, up to their knees – and undid the large door of the bird shed and had to take the birds out, mainly by hand. When the birds couldn't get back into their home, they perched in the trees close by, then, when the water went down, as soon as the door was open again, they rushed in. I don't think one bird was lost."

"Thank God, Mother, that's very good news!" The Archbishop looked up at the bus. "Mother, your community is waiting for you. I must go back inside the Cathedral, but keep me informed of everything involved, in the legal situation. I've already spoken to our lawyers, also to our Finance Committee. So, you keep me informed from your end, and I'll do the same from here." He took Angelica's arm again and helped her to get back into the bus.

He waited until the bus left, waving to the small group of Sisters as they set out for the long drive back to their home.

As he walked slowly back up the Cathedral steps, the Archbishop silently prayed: Dear God, *if Charles is still alive*, please, please, please let me know. If he is truly dead, as I know he must be, wherever he ended up, please take away this foolish refusal to accept the obviously truthful fact that Charles, Cardinal York is… *dead*.

THE POWER OF THE TOWER

The Prime Minister was being briefed by her private, confidential secretary.

"Prime Minister, I've just had a secret call on our secure line, from the secretary of the Minister of Defence."

The busy Head of State, frowned. "What in heaven's name is wrong now? Who has defected, or how many are now clamouring to be let in; we simply can't take any more!"

"You were nearly right the first time, Prime Minister. Or, at least, that could be the answer to the puzzle."

"What puzzle?"

"Well, St Bede's hospital, in the London docks area, has received a half-drowned man, elderly, but British, they *think*. He'd been found by the Coast Guard yesterday morning. It appears he'd been thrown from a boat earlier in the day."

"Someone trying to enter illegally?"

"It could be, but that would be no problem; we'd fix him up and send him back from wherever he came from.

"However, the secretary said the Minister is worried, as close to where the man was found, the Coast Guard had to chase a Chinese Spy Ship back out; it had been in territorial waters. The Minister thinks the elderly man may have fallen, or been thrown, from the spy ship."

"I see. Yes, that's makes all the difference. Right! Inform the secretary to pass on to his Minister that my advice is to move the, possibly, elderly spy, into protective custody, until we can fully investigate the situation. We would most definitely need to discover his name, and where he actually came from. He should be moved to a secure facility as soon as possible – if he *can* be moved.

"If he's English, as is suggested, then it's our own responsibility; if it's another country, that's easy; we just send him back with a curt note expressing our outrage etc. You know the drill, Robert; we've done this a hundred times."

"One more thing, Robert. Let the Minister know that I must be kept informed as to where this man is, together with all information that has been extracted from him, *at all times*. I cannot be caught by the Press unaware of this character, just in case it turns out to be one of our own who has turned traitor. The Press would have a field day with that!"

The Prime Minister looked up. "Thank you, Robert'. The secretary left the room; the Prime Minister sighed heavily, then turned to the masses of documents on her desk.

She was longing for a good strong cup of tea. She had that tingling feeling, behind the eyes, which often presaged a bout of migraine.

* * *

"Doctor, do you have a minute?" Nurse Travers called softly as she saw the doctor hurrying past. He paused and looked at his patient.

"What is it? Any real change, Nurse?"

"Yes, indeed. His eyes are open nearly all the time now; he is looking around at everything, listening to all that that is being said, and looks a thousand times better than when he was first brought in and now the tubes are out, he's eating well."

"I'm glad of that. I've been told of a special message that's come to us from the Home Office about this man." He lowered his voice, "I think he's more important than either of us thought. There seems to be a suggestion he could be" he again lowered his voice… "a spy!"

"No! Are you serious?" The Nurse was astonished. The doctor nodded.

The nurse was unconvinced. "I simply don't believe it. If he is, he is the most, polite, highly educated, courteous gentleman I've ever attended. So, give me spies every time to nurse, if that's the case."

The doctor was amused and laughed softly. "I suppose, Nurse, spies are not an alien species, nor would they come in all the same shape, size and temperament. There could be polite, well educated, courteous ones, together with rough and surly ones. I don't know anything about them; I've never had one before – that I'm aware of, I mean.

He put on a comical face. "I suppose I *could* have, Nurse. They wouldn't have *that* listed under the normal listing of occupations, would they?" They both laughed softly.

"But, to be serious, now." The doctor continued. "The Defence boffins are arranging for a police guard while he is here – he's going to be moved to a secure facility, as soon as we give him the OK. They also want to know this man's name and where he was born. Has he said anything about that?"

"Yes, he has. I don't know what to make of it."

"What was it?"

"Well, whenever I ask his name he says: 'Charles, Antonin, Alexis Dimitri Brendokocov'. And, maintains he was born in Reykjivik…That's Iceland, isn't it?"

"Yes, but… 'Brendokocov', that sounds Russian, doesn't it?" The doctor wrote down the information; he'd pass that on later.

He looked at the nurse again. "Of course, he *could* be Russian; they look, really, the same as Angle-Celtic English do.

"But Reykjivik? What the hell were his parents doing in that bleak, dark country? Has he said anything about that?"

"Yes, he has. I asked the same questions. He said his mother and father were in the Diplomatic Corps; he was born in the airport as they were leaving the country, having finished their assignment there."

"Well, that could explain Reykjivik. But if it is true, then it should be fairly easy to verify the name. I assume that diplomats would have to be thoroughly vetted. But, *which Diplomatic Corps*? *That's* the real question. Could be foreign diplomats.

"We'll have to go easy here, Nurse, we could easily find ourselves in a hell of a mess. They instructed me to do all we can to find out what on earth he's doing here, in merry old England.

"However, let's concentrate on making him well again. That's our job; we're not agents, interrogators, or servants, of the Defence Minister."

The doctor moved to the bedside and looked at his patient. 'Charles' looked up at him with bright, clear, intelligent eyes and, before the doctor could speak, the patient got in first.

"Doctor, I was not aware we were in China. You do speak English, don't you?" The Nurse was embarrassed and went to reply. The doctor put up his hand to prevent her from speaking. "Why did you ask? Were you expecting to wake up in another country?"

The patient frowned, irritated at the interruption.

"I don't think I expected anything to be honest. Don't distract me. I wish to complain about the absence of cream with the apple pie last night at dinner. If you are serving apple pie and cream, then ontologically speaking, one aspect of the nature of being, is missing, if the cream is not present. That is perfectly clear I trust."

"I beg your pardon."

"Do you have a hearing problem? So sad, and you so young, too."

The doctor was tired; he'd just come from Theatre and was not in the mood for jokes, no matter how clever they were.

"Well, I do happen to know what 'ontology' means, but I've never thought of using that word in connection with apple pie. I doubt if anyone else has, either…Now, let's stop this nonsense. We need to know your full name and where you came from; so quit being a clever pain in the neck and give us the facts."

"That sounds so vulgar, you could be an American. But then, I've only heard Americans from New York and Chicago speak like an old movie: '*Give me the facts*!' I found the rest of Americans to be far more polite, erudite and courteous than your average Englishman." The doctor refused to be side-tracked this time.

"Forget all that; you're deliberately trying to befuddle me. No mucking about. Now tell me truthfully. Is your name really that collection of Russian names – straight out of a bad Russian novel?"

The patient, hearing this question, paused, obviously thinking deeply… before he ventured to offer a tentative reply.

His voice was suddenly diffident, unsure and worried.

"To be absolutely truthful, Sammy, as I always am to you, I'm not quite sure if it is my real name, or something I read."

"Why did you call me 'Sammy'?"

"I honestly don't know. Isn't it, Sammy?"

"No."

"That's strange. If you are in charge here, what have you done to Sammy?"

"Who's Sammy?"

The patient became agitated. "Something's wrong… somehow." He went to sit up and managed a half-way attempt. "Tell me how old am I? Am I more than twenty?"

The doctor smiled. He then spoke quietly. "Listen to me, carefully. You are a good long way past twenty."

"No! Goodness! Past thirty?" the doctor nodded. "Heavens, do I have any hair left. My father went bald very young, but my mother had a glorious head of hair until she was ninety…" The patient began to sweat.

"Wait a minute, wait a minute! How do I know she was ninety? Is she dead?" The patient became more disturbed and fearful.

"Doctor, what's wrong with me? Why am I here in hospital? Is it a hospital? Why are you Chinese? Is it a Chinese hospital? Have I had an accident?" He closed his eyes. "All I remember is a flood of water, nothing else…No! …… that's not right. I remember *GERTRUDE*? Oh, my dearest Gertrude! Did she make it? Oh, I loved her like a daughter. Is she all right? Quickly, tell me… Doccccccccc…….."

"Nurse, quick he's fainted. Check the blood pressure and pulse immediately. I'll listen to the heart. Quick now…I think he's starting to remember some traumatic event…this could send him straight back into the state he was in when they first brought him in."

Soon, the man's colour came back and he lay quietly, conscious again. However, his eyes were troubled, and his brow was creased with furrows.

The nurse bent over him and bathed his sweaty face with a damp cloth. "Just take it easy, for a moment or two, Charles. I think you've had a very great shock and are starting to remember all that happened to you. Please, don't worry. You are totally *safe* here now. Whatever it was, it's all over now." She helped the elderly man to make himself more comfortable.

"Now, don't be worrying, Charlie, about the doctor being Chinese. Yes, his parents are Chinese, but Doctor was born and educated in England – that's where you are, pet – England…and he's a very kind and famous doctor. He's the main surgeon here and helps us with the very difficult surgical operations and with all our 'mystery' cases."

The elderly man patted the hand of the sympathetic woman.

"You're a good woman, Nurse, and very kind. Would you please tell me your name? I'll give you permission to call me by that familiar name you used; no one else one earth can call me familiar names, except Sammy."

"Charles, my name is Nurse Betty Travers, but, tell me *who is* Sammy? Is he your son?"

"Don't be vulgar, Miss. He is my secretary. At the university."

"Which university?

"The University of Darumbuljka. The Chancellor there is Dr Rafik Abbas."

"Is Darumbuljka a city? Is it in England?"

"Don't be ridiculous. It's in the middle of the desert. Delicious dates there."

"And, you were a Professor there?"

"I was a *Consultant*. Especially, when the camels were newly born or needed extra care."

"Camels?"

"Of course! To ride on. You must be backward here. What do you use?"

The nurse tried to look apologetic. "I'm sorry, Charles, we are a bit backward; we use cars here."

"But what about carbon hand-prints? I've read about those."

"It's 'foot-prints' Charles. Now, my lad, that's enough! I think you're recovering fast; I'm becoming familiar with your game; you are having me on! Let's forget all the silly questions and answers for a little while. I want you to have a little nap and we can talk later."

The nurse smiled at the patient and left the cubicle trying to make sense of that conversation. She hazarded a guess: I bet that's a mixture of true facts and nonsense, all jumbled together.

"Yes," she called to another patient. "I'm coming now."

AN EASTERN PAINLESS MAKEOVER

Charles slept for fifteen minutes and woke in a fright. Where was he, for heaven's sake? He scrambled out of bed aghast to discover he was wearing only a short gown that was open down the back. Where on earth were his undies and his trousers?

He glanced quickly around the curtains. There was no one in sight. He had to find his clothes. Sammy would be angry if he found him like this. How could he get out of this place – whatever it was – without them seeing him? He shrugged. First the clothes, then he'd work out the rest.

Holding, the back of his gown together, he crept along the ward, noticing that most of the other people seemed to be sleeping…perhaps, it was some type of shelter, or refuge, for men. "Strange place", he muttered.

He paused outside one room where the door was open. It seemed to be a change room. He must have left his clothes here.

Taking the first pair of trousers hanging on a hook near the door, Charles found, to his delight, that they fitted perfectly so they were obviously his own. He quickly pulled on the shirt, wondered why he found some difficulty in trying to tie the tie, but managed it eventually, then found a good pair of black shoes which were a little tight, but they looked great. He was happy to see his suitcoat fitted him; it always had been a good fit.

An overcoat was hanging there as well. He thought he'd better take the heavy coat; if he had brought it in, it must mean it's cold outside. He saw the stethoscope hanging on the peg and slung it across his shoulder.

Fully dressed now, Charles, crept softly out of the room and went towards the lift. While he was fingering the long stethoscope over the shoulders of his coat, he found a large name tag on the lapel as well. It had his name displayed in large print: 'Dr Charles Wangchi.'

Charles was surprised. Well, well, well! He didn't know he was Chinese, but then he seemed to have lost his memory of just about everything else so, obviously, he couldn't remember *who* he was, as well. He wondered why he had a Chinese name. Perhaps an ancestor from the Imperial Court of Peking?

How interesting! He was a *medical doctor*! Strange, he couldn't even remember how to put on a band-aid. And, he didn't think he could speak Cantonese, or Mandarin either, for that matter. Oh well; he must have known once. He decided not to bother about that as, doctor and Chinese or not, he had to get out of this place, unobserved, to the shops to buy some underclothing.

What one earth have they done with his undies? Never mind, he'd buy some brand-new ones; he discovered he had quite a large sum of money and cards in the wallet he found in his back pocket. Therefore, he realised he must be a very *wealthy* Chinese doctor, he decided.

He passed a mirror on the way to the lift. He glanced at himself. He had forgotten what he looked like; he didn't *look* very Chinese, he decided…he looked decidedly English. But wait a minute! Just wait a minute! Where did he get all that white hair? He knew that Chinese had back hair! He couldn't have been in hospital for years, could he? Of course not! He'd obviously had a nasty shock of some sort and it had turned his hair white. How weird, but he'd fix than up before he started off on his journey.

His journey? Where was he going? Home of course, he reminded himself. Right, but first he'd need a quick dye job. He couldn't arrive back in China with white hair. They wouldn't recognize him. But first he had to get out of this place, whatever it was.

Just near the mirror was an emergency bell, bright red, with the usual instructions: 'Break the glass if an emergency occurs and push button'. This immediately gave Charles an idea.

Charles followed the instructions carefully.

The air was instantly filled with screaming wails of sirens, fire-doors crashing to, and people were running in every direction, shouting instructions to each other. Charles avoided the lift and walked quickly down the stairs as fast as he could. He was soon in the foyer and taking the stethoscope from around his collar, he held it in his hand and hurried, with a purposeful look, through the doors, as though he was going to an emergency outside the building. People made way quickly for him, as soon as they saw the stethoscope.

He soon found himself outside in the crisp cool air. He was soon ensconced in a taxi, asking the driver to be taken to a discreet men's hair- dresser where he could get attention to his hair; he explained that he had been in an accident and wanted to look his best as he had an appointment with the palace. Then, if the driver would wait, he wanted him to take him to a good shop where he could buy men's clothing.

The taxi had some difficulty in getting around all the emergency vehicles: the ambulances, the fire engines and the police were everywhere.

Even as Charles watched, the Television crews were arriving to take their positions to film the disaster and report on it – whatever it was! He would have like to stay and see what the emergency was, it could have been interesting.

The driver, taking in the very expensive clothes, the name tag and the upper-class expression and voice, kept silent. Soon, Charles found he was being deposited outside a very grand shop, with a liveried man outside to open the door for the customers. The driver was happy to wait; he knew it would be ages and he was longing for a cigarette.

The elegant hair saloon was the equivalent of a millionaire's private apartment. He explained his problem with his hair, was handed over to Eugene, and whisked away, to where they did extraordinary things to his hair and face which, after a long interlude, seemed to have worked wonders.

"It's not too black is it,?" he asked tentatively. Eugene recoiled in horror. "Sir, nobody would ever dream it had ever been any other colour than a natural deep black. You have a wonderful head of hair, sir, and now you look as you should."

When the bill was presented with an almost sleight of hand movement, Charles gasped at the amount. However, he remembered he was very wealthy and paid with one of the credit cards in his wallet. He then went out to find his driver, waiting and whistling, looking at the traffic. Within minutes he was speeding towards his next shop to buy the clothing he needed.

Inside, the clothing shop, the two main colours were Red and Gold. Charles thought it looked magnificent. Charles couldn't remember being in a shop like this in his life before. He whispered to the floor walker what he wanted and was taken to a special section where he was sold, with utter discretion, a dozen pairs of everything he needed.

Charles found, to his surprise that he didn't have any difficulty with English money. He was again shaken by the price and had to have recourse once more to the credit card. He, again, tentatively produced one from the good number of cards in his wallet and had no problems whatsoever. The clothes were placed in a stunning carry bag of superlative quality, with the Royal Crest on the front. He was ready to leave when he realized he'd need a suitcase.

To his delight, he found the store had a special section, called 'Travel' with a by-line: '*Are you sure you have everything you need*?' Charles found he could buy a small leather suitcase, some pyjamas and handkerchiefs, shaving equipment, tooth paste and a few other things he thought he might need.

He also thought it prudent to buy a pair of amber-tinted glare glasses; there could be a problem with the Chinese name. Even though he certainly *must* be Chinese, and it *must* be his name, he was aware he didn't look a bit like the usual ones you meet in London. He also bought a very smart cloth cap shaped like a Kepi and, putting it on thought it looked jauntily dashing. He thought he looked like a French/Chinese colonel on leave from the Foreign Legion. The black side-leavers looked great at the sides of the Kepi.

He paused, as he was about to leave the shop. What had he just thought? ...*he didn't look like the ones you meet in London*...When had he ever seen Chinese in London? ...When? ...He couldn't remember ever being here before! He shook his head vexedly. He had to get home...wait a minute! ... *Where* was home? ... Was it China? ...No, that didn't sound right...wait a minute! ...Rafik – that's where he had to go! To Rafik! ... *Who* the hell was Rafik? ... No, *Stop it*! ...Don't think at all, he counselled himself – you'll go mad if you do! You're going home to Rafik, and that's that!

He hailed another taxi and was soon on his way to the airport. He'd be glad to be back home in the desert of Darumbuljka.

One hour later, Dr Charles Wangchi was on his way to Algeria –

the first leg of his long and complicated flight to, what he believed to be, his desert home.

He'd been hustled through customs in the VIP lounge with only a cursory glance at his passport. Once the officer had noted the famous name; the passport had then been courteously stamped and the official, smiling, waved the passenger through to the moving platform.

The officer thought he must remember to tell his current girlfriend he'd met the famous, wealthy Dr Wangchi; she's be impressed - she was mad about celebrities. He'd tell her the famous doctor was much older than the newspapers pictures indicated; his publicity photos must be air brushed, he decided.

THE SPY HAS FLOWN THE COOP

"Excuse me, PM, for breaking into your office like this..."

"What on earth is the matter, Robert?"

"It's that elderly man they picked up out of the sea. He given the hospital staff the slip and disappeared."

"How on earth did that happen, Robert? There were strict instructions given to keep that man secure..."

"He created a false emergency PM, and caused havoc in the Hospital; there were hundreds of police, emergency workers, ambulances and para-medics involved...It's cost a fortune..."

"How did he get out of his ward..."

"I don't know, but he, not only disappeared; he's taken the Chief Medical Officer - a Dr Charles Wangchi - this man - whoever he is - has taken *the doctor's* clothes and left the doctor without anything other than his undies and his loose medical gown; the castaway's flown the coop."

"Why were all the doctor's clothes available, Robert? Sounds odd to me."

"The doctor had just been in the Theatre with a delicate operation on a critically, badly-burned patient. He had to remove all his clothes - except his undies - even his shoes and socks, and had to wear only disposable scrubs with a gown on top, in order to operate without infecting the patient..."

"I see. Has Security...?"

"Yes, they were the ones who informed us. They insisted you be told at once. They have notified the airports and ships in port, even the railway stations." The Prime Minister closed her eyes, thinking rapidly.

"So, it seems as if he really were a spy then, Robert... a *British* spy, worse luck!

"*But, wait a minute,* Robert! This is just too coincidental: a traitor falling from a *Chinese* Spy vessel, then gone missing from a hospital wearing a *Chinese* doctor's clothes. Something smells here, Robert.

"What do we know about this doctor? This *Wangchi*? They could be in cahoots – I'm inclined to think they must be."

"That's exactly what I asked the Security bods, PM. They told me they have arrested the Chinese doctor and he is at present in the local nick. It appears that he certainly has Chinese parents, but he was born and educated in Britain, so he is a *completely legal, British citizen*."

"Damn!"

Robert went on: "Wangchi's supposed to be an expert surgeon and does honorary Operating Theatre work in the Docks area in hospitals, such as St Bede's. He is also reputed to be worth a fortune."

Robert coughed, slightly embarrassed. "PM, I'm sorry, but you have to know this. Dr Wangchi is a very generous, *financial* patron of the Conservative Party."

The Prime Minister pulled a sour face. "That was all that was needed to ruin my day, thank you Robert." The PM sat up straight.

"Right, there is no way we can cover this up; let it all be out in the open. Notify the Press, Robert. Let it be seen we are exposing a traitor; that we are not trying to cover up anything; that the security of Britain is our main concern, no matter the colour, race, or political associations an individual belongs to."

Robert was writing, in shorthand, as quickly as he could. He looked up when he'd finished. "Shall do, PM, immediately. I'll let the proper authorities know straight away; I'll ask that it be headlines in all the evening papers tonight."

The Prime Minister, gently patted, with a small beautiful handkerchief, the beads of perspiration on her upper lip, careful not to smudge her lipstick.

"Thank you, Robert. Then, would you get me the Chairman of the Cabinet and ask him to see me *immediately* for emergency discussions on how we are to handle this situation. The only thing I can see, at the moment, is to make the most of this opportunity to deflect attention from the spy to, allegedly, his associate, this Wangchi character."

Robert nodded and left the room hurriedly, his face anxious with worry. He had tremendous affection for the Prime Minister, and he knew, full well, how the *others* would use this information against her.

It was less than ten minutes later that Robert received word from Security that there was a Dr Charles Wangchi en-route to Algeria. The plane was due to land in 47 minutes. He informed the PM immediately.

She asked him the same question that he had asked Security: 'How the hell did he get through Heathrow without a passport?'

She also demanded the Minister for all Ports to begin immediately an investigation into the matter and to announce to the Press an investigation is already underway; she knew from bitter experience it was better to get in first.

A NEW MIDDLE EAST CRISIS

Well, the plane *should* have landed in Houan Boumediene airport in Algeria in 47 minutes, but during the last ten minutes of the flight, it developed problems in the second engine. The plane began to shudder badly. People started to scream with fear.

Charles slept quietly throughout the whole episode.

Ground control ordered the plane to turn away from its flight path and try to see if it could get to Libya – they had better facilities there to deal with emergencies. The plane turned slightly, and keeping at the lowest safest altitude possible, reduced its speed, and limped its way to the main airport in Libya.

Through the expertise of the pilots, the plane landed safely in Libya as Charles woke up, very surprised, but nor alarmed, to be in a country he didn't expect.

The passengers were greatly relieved to have been landed safely but found themselves with another problem. They were permitted to exit the plane, but were not permitted to leave the departure lounge; they had no visas for Libya.

The men and women sat in angry groups watching other flights depart to other countries, but none back to Algeria.

Charles would have liked to stay in Libya for a while to see the sights but, after being bitten twice on the neck, by bees, as he'd headed for the Holding Room, he decided it was too dangerous. Besides being slightly painful, the stings became horribly itchy. He'd scratched all the way across the tarmac. Inside the department lounge, he applied water to the bites; gradually the irritation died down, but the marks on his neck remained bright-red and angry-looking.

Charles watched in dismay as plane after plane left. How was he to get to Darumbuljka now? Just then, an announcement came for passengers to Romania to board their flight.

Several people, from their flight, got up and joined the passengers to Romania; Charles heard some passengers say it was easier to get a plane home from Romania, than to remain where they were.

There was quite a crowd of people now milling about to join the Romanian plane. Charles – as was his wont – without conscious thought, automatically followed the moving column of people.

He showed his passport and explained his position to the two officials who were arguing with one another. One of them nodded to Charles and went on with his conversation; his eyes skimming over the name of the passenger; he then asked if Charles intended staying more than ninety days. Charles said he didn't. The friendly official assured him there was no problem then; he'd not need a Visa for Romania if that was the case.

The officer smiled, and told Charles to 'Hop Aboard', which he did with alacrity. The two men returned to their argument; it was about football, as far as Charles could make out.

BOUDICCA TO THE RESCUE

"Sir there is a woman – a Ms Elizabeth Travers – here to ask about our prisoner, Dr Wangchi."

"Is she related to the man?" The Superintendent asked, brusquely.

"No, sir. However, she is a nurse and works with the doctor at St Bede's. I thought she could be useful."

"I think you're right. Yes, bring her in, Sergeant. This could be interesting."

Nurse Travers had come straight from the hospital, so was still wearing her uniform. She was in a rage and didn't care who knew it. As she entered the office, the Superintendent began to speak; she, immediately, shouted him down.

"Are you entirely insane?" She barked at him. "To arrest one of the finest doctors in Great Britain! One who is immensely powerful; who will have you in court for every charge that his lawyers can think up." She leaned over the shaken man.

"Just tell me, what is the charge against Dr Wangchi? He and I were working on the same patient. He returned to the Operating Theatre, and I to the others in ICU – where I am the Head Nurse – when the emergency bell went off. We have strict protocols to follow in such a situation, and my first duty was to get the patients out, if I possibly could. I came back to the special patient, and the patient had disappeared. That's the end of the whole story, so what the hell has Dr Wangchi to do with it?"

The Superintendent went to speak...Again the angry young woman beat him to it.

"And, if you're thinking of saying I should have only concentrated on the new patient, you can go to hell! Every patient in that ward is in a critical state, and each is as important as the one you're after." She drew a deep breath. "Again, I'll ask you. What is the doctor's crime? What has he been charged with? Why are you holding him, like a common prisoner?"

"I think, Ms Travers, it's the *name.* You see... the Government believes this man is connected, in some way, with something about a spy..."

"Oh yes, from possibly a Chinese Spy Ship and the patient, whose name was, we think, 'Charles', was thought to be have been thrown from that ship."

"Well there *was* a coincidence... The Chinese ship, the doctor's name..." weakly suggested the Superintendent.

"I see, so this is a case of Racial Discrimination is it? Are you aware, you moron, that Charles Wangchi was born and educated in England, and is therefore a completely legal, *British, Citizen*? His parents have been here all their lives as well. His father is the Patron of several Royal Societies; is invited to Royal banquets at the palace, and you stick his son in a filthy dungeon...WHY? You...are...a...*FOOL*!"

The policeman began to wipe his face with his handkerchief. "He's not in a dungeon, Ms..."

"I demand to see him...immediately. He has no clothes; the patient stole all his clothes; doctor had nothing to put on when he came out of Theatre. I rummaged around and found an old pair of trousers and a shirt, but we had no shoes, so he's in a pitiful state."

She waved a finger in front of the Superintendent's face. "Just wait until I spill all this to the Press! Your name – which I see on your door is 'Sample' – well, let me tell you something, buster --tonight, on Television, the British public will all be hearing about 'Simple Sample', and laughing their heads off."

Betty Travers stood up straight. "I'm waiting…waiting to see him. Get moving buster, your whole career depends on it…." The superintendent pushed a button on his desk. The Sergeant appeared immediately. He stood to attention before the great man.

The Superintendent tried to speak with authority but failed dismally.

"Sergeant would you please escort Ms Travers to see the Pris… the gentleman… in cell number six. And, please ask Sergeant Thelma Black to just check the visitor's handbag. That will be sufficient." He stood up. "Thank you, Ms Travers, would you kindly go with the Sergeant now. Thank you."

As soon as Betty had left the room, the Super hastily rang headquarters. What the hell was he supposed to do *now*?

* * *

They had placed Charles Wangchi in a cell on his own. As soon as Betty entered the cell, she ran to the bewildered and dishevelled man and wrapped her arms around him, her tears flowing freely.

After a moment, she realised what she had done, and apologized with gasping sobs. Charles moved forward and held her again.

"You can't realise Betty how precious it is to see somebody who is not terrified that I'm here to blow up something, or learn the secrets of the latest bomb, or submarine or, anything." Betty gently released his arms.

"Charles," she spoke in a quiet, serious manner. "We cannot

waste time. Let me know quickly the number of your solicitor's and your parents' phones. I could let both groups know. We must act fast. Your solicitor has to get you out of here…and quickly too. All the Press has been alerted."

"God help us! My mother will have a fit with the shame; my father will be very angry. Neither of them liked my working in the Docks area, and for this to happen…"

"Charles, we must keep to the sensible things. Did you have much cash in your wallet, or cards… those sorts of things...anything that could have been of use to the villain who stole them?"

"Betty, I had every credit card I possess in it and about a thousand pounds in cash…"

"God in Heaven help us! You were a thief's answer to prayer! Your solicitor must stop the cards immediately. Has he the numbers of the cards?" Charles nodded. "What the hell were you carrying all those explosive things around with you? No, don't answer that; that has nothing to do with me. Tell me… besides the cash and the cards, anything else that could be used?"

"Betty, I know you've going to scream, but my passport was in my back pocket – I needed it for identification for a project I was working on…"

"Dear God, you truly were a thief's best friend…Ooooh!"

"What?"

"I suddenly realised how that could be twisted against you. Can I tell the solicitor that?"

"Betty, tell him anything you can think of; I don't know whether I'm on my head or my heels." The man sat on the edge of his bunk. "I don't know now whether to laugh, or to cry. I've never been in such a ridiculous situation before in my life. It's like being back at boarding school in the first year and being called: 'Charlie the Chink'.

"It's all because of the blasted name, Betty; that what it's all about – they've linked me to that rotten Chinese Spy boat because of the name!"

"Charles, I brought a notebook and I have my ball-point in my uniform pocket. Just give me the numbers quickly. I could be thrown out of here in a moment, so let's not waste one moment more."

For the next seven minutes, Betty wrote as Charles dictated. Just as she was finishing, the cell door opened, and the Sergeant appeared.

"Excuse me, Ms, but I'm afraid you have to go; the Internal Security Department has advised us that you are not to visit this person apprehended, until he has been cleared. I'm sorry, Ms."

Betty shook hands in a dignified manner with the doctor.

"Doctor, I shall see that all England knows of what has been done to you; that our homeland, yours and mine, should do this to you, makes me ashamed. Goodbye and God keep you safe."

The doctor was genuinely moved and spoke solemnly. "Nurse Travers, thank you for coming to me in this disgraceful situation. I cannot and will not forget this kindness." He shook hands holding the young woman's hands tightly.

Betty followed the Sergeant out and, once outside, ignored both police and the Press, with total indifference and made a bee line for the taxi rank. She got into a cab and was driven swiftly back to the hospital. She knew she could have free and *private* access to the telephones there. She had completed all that Charles Wangchi had asked of her within twenty minutes.

As she sat still, Betty recalled the phone call to the doctor's mother. In her mind she heard again the shrieks of anguish of the elderly Mrs Wangchi when Betty had explained Charles' situation.

The huge spurt of energy she had used in her defence of

Charles was starting to sap away. Betty was only a young woman, worn out after a long and difficult shift in the ward. She put her head down on the desk and wept for the doctor she adored.

BETTY MOVES TO MAYFAIR

Fifteen minutes later, Betty received an urgent call on the hospital intercom to come to the Main Office. She responded quickly to the call wondering what new and horrible disaster had been brought to them this time.

Arriving in the main office, Betty was confronted by a very tall, beautifully dressed, regal, elderly man of Chinese appearance standing with his chauffeur, waiting for her. The chauffeur introduced Mr Wangchi senior to the embarrassed nurse, and she shook the beautifully manicured hand that was extended to her.

"Ms Travers, I have spoken to Management and they have agreed to a proposition I have to make to you," the man spoke gravely and courteously. "I would like you to come with me now to my home and, personally, take care of my wife during this terrible time. She is in a terrible state, our only child is now in… in …jail! ... I find it difficult to even say that word.

"I have heard from the Police how valiantly you have defended my son. I would like you to come to my home and be with us in this our hour of need."

Betty didn't know how to answer. Yes, she would like to be with these gracious people, but she lived in a council flat with her widow mother. She had no idea how to live with the rich and famous. She muttered her embarrassment; her ignorance of elegant living…

Her objections were cut short.

"Nurse Travers, we live in a grand house and, yes, everything is very beautiful and expensive, but we are just two elderly people living in a state of bewilderment; we don't know what to do, or where to turn. Please, come to us; we are very, very ordinary, simple, people."

He turned to his chauffeur. "Jake here will assure you that you will find no difficulty with us. Yes, he is my chauffeur, but he is also my righthand man. I couldn't do without him; he will explain anything to you that you might need to know." He took Betty's hand again.

"Look, I'm going to sit down over there…not feeling too well, actually. You talk her into it, Jake." He bowed to Betty and went to a soft chair against the wall.

Betty and Jake Higgs looked at each other. Jake was smiling.

"Not to worry, love. My folks live in a council flat as well," laughed Jake. "These people are, indeed, truly good, simple, people and they certainly need you. If you can, please come, I'm at my wits end trying to cope with both of them – they're utterly distraught."

The young man then grinned, and said: "Besides that, Betty, the food's bloomin' marvellous."

Betty laughed. "In that case, Jake, I'll come," she finally agreed. "Just drive me home for some decent clothes and I'll be ready."

OUT FOR THE COUNT!

In the plane, which Charles had discovered, was heading to Transylvania, he found, in the racks in front of him, reading matter was available. It had mainly been chosen for tourists. Charles picked through some of the material, not really interested, until he came to a copy of Bram Stoker's book on 'Dracula'. He vaguely remembered reading about vampires before, somewhere. This was interesting; so that's where he was heading now, Transylvania: the land of Count Dracula! Fancy that!

Vampires lived on blood, other people's blood, Charles strangely remembered, and once they had taken blood from a person, that person became a vampire as well, and so the cycle went on. Charles read on, intrigued. I wonder what blood tastes like? he shuddered. His mind started to wander; for a moment his mind flew to Sammy.

Charles momentarily felt a severe sense of loss; of bereavement. Sammy – whoever he was, and wherever, he had known him – had been like a son to him. He wondered where he was now. Perhaps he was dead? Perhaps a vampire got him? But then, he would be a Vampire himself by now and dangerous.

He shook his head. No, he wouldn't believe it! Sammy would never be dangerous to him; even if he were a Vampire. He would be prepared to undergo the test of letting Sammy bite his neck and drawing blood, to prove Sammy was a full human being, not a monster. But… even if he has become a vampire then he would do his best to find the blood he needed to survive; he owed him that much. *Why*? …He shook his head. He couldn't remember, but he knew *he did*!

Charles rubbed the bites on his neck suddenly aware of the slight pain. Good God! Have I already been bitten? Oh dear! I could already be a vampire! He was feeling hungry as well – he needed to eat! Oh dear! He looked up at the passenger next to him, a fat, surly brute of a man, with a thick neck.

No, he couldn't do it! He couldn't bite *his* neck! You never knew what you might catch from someone like him! He doesn't look as if he had washed this morning – dirty fellow!

This being a vampire, was a difficult business; it was more complicated than he had thought. Did it *have* to be blood? Why not a nice bun with lots of cream? Well, he could try and see if that would do…with, perhaps, some fish and chips, as seconds? Worth trying, anyhow. He'd try that first; if it worked, he then wouldn't need the blood.

His mind flew back to Sammy who could possibly be a vampire.

No, he must be dead, he decided. Most of the people he vaguely remembered were now dead. Or, who knows? Sammy could be a 'big shot' by now; Sammy was a very bright young bloke when he first employed him.

Wait a minute! *Wait a minute*! *EMPLOYED* him? For, *WHAT*! Charles started to perspire in his agitation, so forced himself to concentrate on the book he was reading…vampires…yes, Dracula…nice chap, Dracula…royal blood…He began to doze scratching slightly at the irritation on his neck.

The plane, making a bumpy landing in Targu Mures, woke Charles in fright. He followed the crowd from the plane to the custom desk. He was jostled from behind and turned around indignantly, to discover he had been robbed; his passport and wallet had been stolen! He needed to attract attention quickly otherwise the robber would get away.

"Help, help! He shouted in a loud voice, going through a pantomime of searching his pockets for the stolen items.

He was quickly surrounded by custom and security police. He had to work hard to convince them that he only spoke English, so they hurriedly sought an English-speaking officer.

The officials at first thought this was a familiar hoax, but the sight of Charles was intimidating: he was elderly, wore magnificent clothes and had very expensive luggage, which all spoke in his favour.

The official, who spoke English, informed Charles he would have to go to the Embassy in Bucharest; that was the only place which could help him. However, as he had been the victim of a crime while in their country, the airport would arrange for him to take the next flight to Bucharest and a car would be made available to take him to the English Embassy. This would cost Charles nothing and the English Embassy would supply the rest of his needs.

Charles was asked to sit quietly in the waiting room. He was bitterly disappointed; he had not been able to visit Dracula's castle; the Count might have been waiting for him there. They could have been photographed together; Rafik would have been interested in that!

A man came around with a tray selling silly little, cheap, imitation false fangs for tourists. Charles couldn't resist, and finding some coins in a side pocket, bought a number if these. He then put the fangs in his mouth settling them comfortably over his front teeth.

He was totally unaware of the sensation he was causing.

People passing by, took one look at him, saw the bite marks on his neck and hurried away as quickly as possible. Some people actually gave muffled screams! He couldn't understand it when an elderly woman dragged her grandchild away from him in terror, speaking quickly, loudly, and incomprehensively to Charles, while blessing herself non-stop.

A young bold, somewhat vulgar young man, reading a trashy novel, which Charles saw had a near-naked woman on the front cover, plumped himself down next to the cardinal.

"What's it taste, like?" he asked rudely. Charles thought the young chap was an uncouth lout, but at least, this lout *did* speak in English.

"I beg your pardon! I don't understand," replied Charles.

"Oh, come off it; we all know what you are?"

"How interesting; then you know more than I do. This must be the result of your extensive College Education. What am I?"

"You're a vampire, that's what you are! You've got the marks on your neck." The vulgar lout spat on the floor. "Now, don't avoid the question. I'm not afraid of you. So, go ahead, tell me. What does the blood taste like?"

Charles, even if he had lost his memory, was a highly intelligent being with a quick and agile mind. He looked at this youth. It truly was fascinating he thought: the rotters were easily identified, no matter which country they come from. This chap needed his backside tanned, or a quick bout with Sammy in the Ring – whoever Sammy might be, and whatever Sammy was doing in a 'Ring'! Perhaps, Sammy worked in a circus ring? Could that be the answer?

"Come on, spill the beans, pop. I'm waiting to know."

"And I *want* you to know", Charles replied courteously. "I think the only way to really show you what it tastes like is to let you actually taste some." The youth looked a little startled. Charles went on.

"So, if you come a little closer, I'll bite you and draw a small amount of blood – about two litres should be enough – then I'll spit it out into a basin then you can drink it. It's really quite nice – different, sort of spicy." Charles made a swift grab at the man's collar, pulled him close, opened his mouth to reveal the fangs which protruded down over his front eye teeth, and moved his head as if to bite savagely.

The young man shrieked in terror, tore himself away and ran for his life, screaming his head off.

A handful of people, including some officials nearby, began clapping the old gentleman. Charles looked up, removed the teeth and started to laugh. Soon the whole group were laughing. This old foreign man was a wise man, they decided. He knew how to deal with louts. The group crowded around Charles shaking his hand and wishing him well. Charles had no idea in the world what they were saying, but aware of the good-will, responded happily.

In a conversation, later, with an English-Speaking official, Charles was informed the youth was well known to the police; he had been before the Magistrate several times for pickpocketing at the airport.

Very soon after this, Charles was taken to join another flight which took him away from Transylvania – and Count Dracula – and deposited him in the picturesque city of Bucharest – the home of the English Ambassador.

Charles was smiling happily; he was looking forward to seeing Bucharest.

Meanwhile, the thief who had robbed Charles, flew on to *Moscow* using Charles' passport in the name of Dr Charles Wangchi.

THE SPY'S IN MOSCOW, OR IS HE?

The Prime Minister raised her weary head as Robert again hurried into her private office.

"All right! Tell me where the wretched man is *now*!" She snapped at the young secretary.

"I'm sorry, PM, I don't know what his caper is. He been to Romania and now we've had a secret message that he's landed in *Moscow*."

"So, this could indicate that he's working for both China *and* Russia?"

Robert nodded his head sadly. "It's beginning to look that way. God alone knows where he'll turn up next." He turned his head away, listening. "Excuse me PM, my confidential line is ringing."

Robert dashed out of the office, only to reappear three minutes later. "PM, the doctor's been shot in the airport of Moscow... actually shot dead...."

"He's *dead*? Any details?"

"Only that the man shot, was using a false name of a famous English doctor but was well known to the police there; he was considered so dangerous that there were standing orders to shoot him on sight, if he ever returned to the country. So now we have three 'Dr Wangchis.'"

The Prime Minister chewed on her pen. "There is the real man in our prison; the common thief, well known to the police shot dead in Moscow and then we have the spy, posing as Wangchi, apparently aimlessly wandering the world; on whose passport I cannot even guess."

"So," she added wearily, "we're still stuck with him; that is, with the spy at large?" She sat up straight, her eyes startled.

"Robert, could this mean '*our* Dr Wangchi' – the one in our prison – is *INNOCENT*?" She actually shuddered at the possibility of the colossal blunder she had made!

"I'm afraid he could be, Prime Minister! I think we've made a terrible mistake. Regarding the other one, the renegade British spy who's wandering the world, I'll let you know the minute I find any news of the travelling man who's caused all the trouble."

"I think I should step down; I don't think I can cope with any more of this." She closed her eyes. "Thank you, Robert. We have to find him somehow or other; they're giving me hell for failing to do so."

The PM cradles her chin in her hand. "I think this is bringing on a migraine."

THE PRESS TO THE RESCUE

Well, the one and only *real* Charles Wangchi was in a more comfortable cell than he had been before, and wearing good clothes, not prison garb now, but was still staying at the expense of Her Gracious Majesty. He also had been allowed books and study material to be brought in to him.

The young doctor had, through his solicitor's influence, been given the permission to have Nurse Betty Travers visit him twice weekly. Their relationship had travelled from Doctor to Nurse, from her concern for the innocent victim and to become his first, and most fervent, supporter… to something that looked much more intimate.

Betty thought, as did Charles, that they were falling rapidly in love.

They used only first names now; all formality gone. Betty, now living in the house of Charles' mother and father, was able to bring the prisoner all the news he wanted so much to hear about his parents.

Betty had brought Charles' mother once, but they had both decided not to do that again; she had cried throughout the visit and was clearly in a terrible state at seeing their only child a prisoner – one who was called a 'spy', one who was derided – a thing to be cast away.

This was her 'boy': her greatest source of pride, her assurance that, finally, she and her husband were fully accepted by the English people.

The very day the Prime Minister had been briefed by Robert on the latest developments, Betty and Charles were seated at the little table in the visitor's room. They held hands across the table. They were pondering again the strange case of the nearly drowned elderly man they had cared for.

"Do you know what, Charles?" Betty asked. "I still cannot believe all this outrageous 'paper-talk' about him being a master spy, a traitor to England and in league with just about everything journalists can think up."

"Then, *who* was he, Betty?" Charles asked wonderingly.

"Don't laugh dearest, but I think he was just a highly educated elderly man who had undergone some frightful experience, lost his memory, woke up in hospital and when we weren't looking, tried to escape. He took your clothes, saw the label and thought that must be his name and those were his clothes."

"What about all those names he gave us? Were they real?"

She laughed. "Possibly, but I doubt it very strongly. I think it's something he's read, and it's stayed in his head. The only thing I can be sure of is that his first name is Charles. He responded so automatically to *that* it has to be his own name."

"You could be right, Betty. You know, from the first time I saw him, I was unsure whether he was English, or not. *I don't think he actually is British.*"

"Well, if that's the case, Charles, we could do something about that, couldn't we? We have the photo of him from hospital. Could your legal team circulate that photo to all the main papers in the English-reading countries in the world? Or," she added, "where English papers are available."

Betty elaborated on her idea. "You know, Charles; those

photos you see in newspapers, with a caption saying: 'Do you know this man?' We've all seen those."

"That's a sensible and practical suggestion, Betty. I'll get that moving this afternoon; the head lawyer will be here in an hour, I think. We could have all that done for tomorrow morning newspapers."

"Well, I'd better skedaddle then, love." Betty leaned over the desk, gave the prisoner a quick kiss and knocking loudly on the door for the guard, to open the door, gave one last wave to the doctor, and left the prison.

Betty felt more optimistic with the idea of the photo. If it was sent all round the world, *someone, somewhere*, MUST recognize their mystery patient.

THE TOWN OF YORK IS THE TALK OF THE CROWN

Charles sat waiting for the Ambassador. The waiting room was sumptuously furnished: the chairs with a rich golden material, while the walls were painted a deep royal red with splendid reproductions of some of England's finest paintings in gold frames.

It all felt strangely familiar to Charles; he wondered why. As far as he knew, he had never, in his life, been in Romania before. But who knows? Perhaps he had.

He shook his head in real distress. Who was he, really, for heaven's sake? He began to doubt he had ever been a doctor of any nationality - but a *Chinese* medical doctor? No, he wasn't Chinese; he was nearly sure of that – the whole thing didn't make sense.

However, the name Charles Wangchi certainly did seem familiar to him in some way or other. In his mind, Charles linked the name with a very pretty young woman whose name was …? Suddenly, he *knew* the name! It was Betty…Betty… something… *Betty TRAVERS*! He had been in bed somewhere… He had…

His attention was distracted by some loud shouts from the office of the Ambassador.

A Secretary rushed out of the office, excused himself to

Charles, then hurried through to another office, where he was heard speaking rapidly in a foreign language, obviously Romanian. Telephones seemed to be ringing throughout the building.

The door to the main office opened. The ambassador walked slowly towards Charles, silently studying the man before him carefully. Charles stood up and bowed slightly to the tall. grey haired. military looking man.

"Excellency, thank you for coming to my aid; I don't really know what is happening to me..." The tall, elegant man waved aside the thanks.

"I'm sorry. I don't know how to address you, Sir, whether you are the missing Dr Wangchi, or not. There have been certain people, including the Head of the Police Force here, who think they know who you actually are...Tell me, are you English, or not?"

Charles' brow, furrowed. "Your Excellency, I'm not sure... not sure what I am, or...*who* I am." He stood up and faced the important man. "May I ask your name, sir?"

"Of course, forgive me for not telling you when I first spoke to you. I am Sir Malcolm Sparks, my family come from York...."

There was a piercing shriek from Charles:

"*YORK! YORK! YORK!*" He looked at the Ambassador and shouted: "THAT'S WHO I AM!"

"*WHAT?*" asked Sir Malcolm. Charles, in his overwhelming joy and relief, wrapped his arms around the startled man. The ambassador tried to shake off the man, whom he thought was obviously demented.

"*WHAT ON EARTH ARE YOU DOING? What is wrong, man? Are you ill? ... JOHN,*" the man shouted urgently. "JOHN! *Get security*!"

He turned back to Charles, taking his arm firmly. "*What on earth is the matter? Are you all right*?"

Receiving no answer, the ambassador rushed to the bell on the wall. Pushing the bell, he shouted as soon as he heard his secretary's voice. "John, ring for the Nurse instantly, I think the man's having a fit, or a stroke."

Charles stood up straight, hands outstretched; his face radiant.

"No, no stroke, Sir Malcolm! ...*I THINK I KNOW WHO I AM!* When you mentioned '*York*' it all came surging back to me.'

"I am Charles...York! No! ...Wait! There's something missing from the middle space......the middle name is missing."

Charles then frightened the Ambassador, by letting out a terrible, long, drawn-out wailing sound, then clapped his hands to the sides of his head and swayed on his feet. "Dear God in Heaven. *HOW COULD I HAVE FORGOTTEN THAT*!

"Sir Malcolm, I know *who* and *WHAT* I am..."

He grabbed hold of the ambassador's hand. "Sir...you won't believe this...I *can't believe it myself*...I am 'Charles... *CARDINAL*... York! I am a Catholic Cardinal of the Latin Rite of the Church...could that possibly be the solution to the mystery of who I am?

"I can't believe I could have forgotten...But, what have I done? I've stolen a doctor's clothes; I've been travelling everywhere, not knowing who I was, but thinking I must be, this Doctor Wangchi... Oh! Dear Lord! Poor Sammy! He must have thought I was dead... Oh! No, I can't bear it... I'm...*I'm...I... never intended...*"

Charles swooned, crumpled and fell to the floor, as several Embassy staff, including the nurse, came rushing into the room. The Ambassador shouted: "*Notify the PM at once! We now know who the man is!*"

MURPHY'S LAW IN ACTION

'If something can go wrong; it will go wrong'

The Prime Minister held her head in her hands. "I can't believe it! I simply can't. *A Cardinal*! ... He couldn't have been a simple priest! ... Oh no! He has to turn out to be *a Cardinal of the Church!*

"Robert, if it's true, they'll crucify me for this...." The woman looked all in; she looked appealingly at her young secretary. "Robert, advise me. What on earth can I do? This could bring down the government. Can I retrieve anything out of this mess?"

Robert was upset. He genuinely liked his prime minister; he belonged to the same party she led. He sat, without permission, pondering this situation, his eyes tightly closed. Finally, he had an idea.

"What about...a special invitation to a Reception given by you, to this doctor and his parents and this nurse - can't remember her name - the one who's been fighting for him and driving the police force crazy?"

"Yes, that's an idea...we'll do that. What was the swanky doctor doing down in the Docks area in the first place, Robert?"

"Apparently, it was his charity work for the down and outs. He mainly worked at St Bede's hospital. They get all the drunks, druggies, the homeless poor when they are found by the police. It is a wonderful place; I've actually been there. For all I know I could have met the famous doctor..."

The PM interrupted her secretary. "Robert, you've given me an idea. What about a special grant to that particular hospital, with...perhaps...a special coverage in the newspapers on the splendid work they do there – with plenty of photos? And, of course, a special award for the good Doctor, as well?" She then looked straight at the young man opposite her.

"There's absolutely no need, Robert, to mention that I've never heard of the place, nor the doctor, before in my life."

Robert laughed. "Understood, clearly, PM." He stood up. "Now, do you want me to get all that underway? I personally think we should act as quickly as we can – get in, before the other side can start their attack."

"Yes, but first get onto the Commissioner of Police, and the Chief Constable, to extend their heart-felt apologies for the misunderstanding. Advise all those at the prison their heads will roll, if they don't outdo themselves, in their courtesy, to the doctor.

"Send my sincere and heart-felt congratulations to the doctor's parents that this terrible ordeal is over; word it as if I had nothing to do with it. Then, fit in a time for the reception – make it as soon as possible, with all the Press present. Notify the cabinet: I only want the main ones to be present – not the lot; it would be too big a crowd. We should try to make this as *intimate* a reception as possible, but with all the Press you can muster up.

"*Stress that Robert*! *All the Press*!" The PM thought for a moment, then went on.

"Fix up the article on St Bede's: perhaps you can get that good young journalist Brian Wallis to write that...he's good, and notify that department that prepares all the awards – I can never remember which one it is – we'll think up something appropriate: perhaps a special medal for exemplary medical services to all in need? Something like that!

"Right! When you've done all that, give me a list of the people you think should be at the reception for the doctor and his parents.... Do you have all that? Off-load as much as you can on the other special office personnel."

Robert had been writing speedily in his impeccable shorthand as the PM was talking. He looked up and nodded. The Prime Minister began to relax a little.

"Well, we've done what we could. Now, I have another problem. When you've finished all that work on Wangchi, come back here.

"We'll then have to work out a plan, for that wretched problem of the sewage malfunction, in that repulsive Public Housing tower block, we built. We must know all the gruesome details of that. At the next meeting of the House of Commons, they'll give me hell over that debacle."

She pulled a sour face. "Why on earth do people keep shoving things down the loo? You'd think they'd have more sense."

Robert stood erect as the PM spoke, then nodded and left the room. Talk of toilets had reminded him: he decided to dash off there now; in this job you never knew when you would have the time, and when you wouldn't.

RECALLED TO LIFE

Charles Cardinal York came to, and found he was lying on top of a bed, with a doctor placing a stethoscope against his chest. His eyes opened in wonder as he saw the group of men around his bed.

The Ambassador came and stood where Charles could see him clearly.

"Your Eminence, I want to introduce these gentlemen to you just so you won't be fearful. There's nothing whatsoever to fear now you have recovered your memory. Now, if you remember, my name is..."

"Sir Malcolm Sparks from York, and you are the English Ambassador, here in Bucharest, for all Romania," concluded Charles. Sir Malcolm clapped happily.

"Well, done Eminence! You have perfect recall, thank God," cried the Ambassador. "Now on my right is ..."

"Good God! It's Porky Peterson! Porky, I'm delighted to see you. I thought you were dead..." The Ambassador was embarrassed and coughed loudly. "Eminence, I take it you know his Grace, the Catholic Archbishop and Apostolic Nuncio for Romania."

"Well, well! Is that what he is? Well, you couldn't have a better man. Terrible appetite, though – ate twice as much as any other student in the University and never put on an ounce. Wasn't fair we thought."

The Nuncio blushed scarlet, as the Ambassador struggled on: "And next to him we have the very clever Journalist who, searching the English newspapers spotted your picture, and matched it with the ones that were taken when you came from the plane which brought you here from Transylvania."

The young man flushed with embarrassment; he was already planning his next big article, on the solution to the international mystery, of the man with no name.

"Could I please see the photo from the newspaper?" Charles asked. The young journalist came forward and showed the photograph. Charles was aghast!

"Why am I wearing civilian clothes?" Charles, in his agitation, sat on the side of the bed. "Have I left the Church? Have I been laicized? Please God, say that isn't true! I couldn't bear to think I've given scandal…Why? Please tell me why I'm wearing those shocking clothes?"

The Ambassador came forward and put his hand on the elderly man's shoulder.

"Well, that brings me to your last visitor, Eminence. I want you to meet Peter Bruges. Peter is the Head of the Police in the whole of Romania and he has been involved in your disappearance, and your bewildering journeying all round the world, in someone else's name and his clothes and belongings…"

"Sir Malcolm," spluttered the Cardinal. "I've never stolen anything in my entire life…."

"Good gracious me, Eminence, perish the thought!" cried the ambassador, horrified. "No, you *did* take the clothes and the other belongings, but you had forgotten who you actually were, and you thought they were your own clothes. That's why you're wearing those clothes."

"But, what about the poor man whose clothes I took? What did he do; he would have had nothing to wear…"

"I'm sorry to say, Sir, that he actually was put in jail…"

"NO! ………. That is terrible! I must throw myself on his mercy. Who was he, some poor, homeless man that I have robbed?"

"Actually, he was one of the most famous doctors in England and immensely wealthy."

"And, I put this important man in prison, and stole all his belongings? I can see a long period in prison ahead of me, and an even longer one in Purgatory, when I die." Charles was near to tears in his distress. He looked up at the Nuncio.

"Could you rustle up something for me to wear, Porky? Doesn't matter which rank it is." He suddenly remembered a difficulty he'd had trying to get dressed in England. "No wonder I had such trouble in tying my tie. It would have been more than 70 years since I wore a tie."

The Nuncio was conferring with both the Police Chief and the ambassador. The Apostolic Nuncio then spoke quietly to Charles.

"Eminence, with the permission of these two gentlemen, I'm going to take you back to the Nunciature and we'll find some proper clothes for you to wear. Then, the Ambassador will arrange for you to be flown back to England, and from there, you can return to your own country."

Charles rose groggily to his feet. He expressed his gratitude and bowed to the Ambassador, then shook hands with the Head of Police and the journalist. He then followed the Nuncio out of the room. The young journalist, whose name was Andrei – so Charles immediately called him 'Andy' – followed the two men and whispered in Charles' ear. Listening carefully, Charles nodded.

The journalist almost ran from the building excited and thrilled. The Cardinal had just granted him exclusive rights to all the press coverages – including the photos – in relation to himself.

Charles had always been a very shrewd operator. He knew, that with that young chap he'd minimise the havoc he had caused, and he might, *just might*, assuage the wrath of the good Dr Wangchi.

'Porky' proved himself a treasure. Back at the Nunciature, he found in his cupboard a fairly old but very clean cardinal's cassock, cape, biretta and cloak. Once dressed as usual again, Charles stood in front of the mirror, then, summonsed the journalist, Andy, to take the first batch of photos – adopting, automatically the pose he had used for the last half century.

It was a beautiful picture and it was *that picture* which featured His Eminence Charles Cardinal York, on the front page of the newspapers across the world the next day, that both, His Grace Archbishop Samuel Spotels, and Mother Angelica saw… with their eyes refusing to take in the astonishing sight… of their '*dead*' cardinal.

In huge black type the message was blazoned: '*HE'S BACK!*'

Sammy and Angelica reacted in different ways. Sammy let out a ferocious yell, and leaping from his chair, frightening both his secretary Monsignor Izzy Grim, and his Vicar General, Fr Jack Okiama.

Sammy then ran around the room shouting: "*I knew it; I KNEW it! Jack, get me a small whisky, quickly; HE'S BACK FROM THE DEAD!*"

And, many miles away, at the Retirement Home, Mother Angelica stared at the picture, rang the emergency bell for the Sisters, held up the newspaper for them to see, then promptly fainted.

Sisters Margaret, Paul, Veronica and Maria, ran to the belfry and began to ring the bells in a positive cascade of sound which poured over the surrounding area.

When all the old clerical residents were informed, the noise in the dining room was astonishing. There were shouts of delight, cheering, yelling and shouting; they kept repeating the same words: 'He's back; he's back; *HE'S BACK!*'

* * *

Back in Bucharest, Sir Malcolm Sparks, the English Ambassador, was in touch with both MI5, and MI6, the Foreign Secretary in the British Parliament, and finally spoke with the Prime Minister herself.

It was from her, that Sir Malcolm learned of the problems that were besetting her Government – and herself – over Dr Wangchi. She confided to her ambassador her problem and her plan to try to rescue the situation.

She told him to see that the Cardinal has everything he needs, especially proper and fitting clothing, and then prepare him for a reception with the victim, the real Dr Wangchi and his parents; then with her and her cabinet, in Westminster. She begged him to get Charles York back to England, as quickly as possible; fix up his passport and anything else he might need to expedite the situation to minimise the benefits this idiotic situation has given to the Opposition.

Sir Malcolm was anxious to do what the PM requested – he owed his position as Ambassador to her, so understood the situation perfectly. He assured the harassed woman that Charles would be on the first flight he could arrange for him. He should be back in London within twenty hours. He would, of course, be flying First Class. When he had the time of arrival of the plane, he would get the Apostolic Nuncio to notify the Cardinal at Westminster to meet Cardinal York when he arrived on British soil.

When the PM broke the connection, Sir Malcolm rang the Nunciature and put the Nuncio in the picture. He was informed, that at that very moment Charles was receiving a haircut and shave and they were doing what they could to get rid of the terrible black dye that had been put in his hair. When all that was over, he was going to be checked by a doctor and then given a good meal as they arranged for the flight.

He added that he was sending the young journalist, Andrei, with Charles; he would be a buffer between the old man and the manic Press who would be ruthless to get all the details of this extraordinary story which had been the headlines for days now.

The two men both agreed that Charles should only be given the chance to say as little as possible – it would be safer, not just for Her Majesty's Government, but for the Church as well.

When all was ready, Charles bid a solemn farewell to both the English Ambassador and the Nuncio, Archbishop 'Porky' Peterson, the Police chief and other dignities, then he, and 'Andy', took their places in the airplane. Charles marvelled at such luxury; he had never flown First Class in all his previous, intentional – and *unintentional* – flights to various countries.

Charles, on the flight, sat next to Andy and the journalist tried to prepare Charles for the whole frenzy of publicity that would erupt as they set down in London. He advised Charles on what to say, how to answer, whom to thank and what they were to do. Charles did try his hardest to remember all the details; he was beginning to find it all rather bewildering.

Andrei was guessing, but he thought it highly likely that Charles would be whisked away, most probably to the British Nunciature. He knew that, once there, Charles would be safe as houses, safe behind the high walls; at least he *hoped* he would.

ANDREI SCORES THE SCOOP!

Arriving at Heath Row Airport, Andy preceded Charles in leaving the plane and showed his credentials to the waiting Officials. He then gestured to Charles, instructing him to wave as he came through the door.

The cardinal shook hands graciously with each of the officials who introduced themselves courteously to him and then let them lead him and his photographer to the VIP lounge where the Papal Nuncio was waiting to receive him.

Andrei took dozens of photos; ignoring the huge gathering of other photographers who were swearing loudly at this upstart, this *Romanian*, who was getting all the best shots.

Charles did not know this Nuncio, so was icily polite. He stood tall and intimidating, offering his hand to be kissed. The Archbishop had no option but to genuflect and kiss the ring of the Fisherman.

Andy was thrilled; this made a terrific shot; he'd be able to syndicate this to newspapers all round the world – he'd make a bundle on this photo alone!

Charles was enjoying every minute of this experience, but the Papal Nuncio quickly informed the cardinal that the car was waiting, and he must come away immediately; they had a difficult few days ahead of them.

With regret, Charles moved towards the exit insisting that he be accompanied at all time by his photographer, and '*Valet*', Andrei. In the long black limousine, with the Vatican flag flying from the bonnet and the Vatican Diplomatic corps insignia discreetly printed on the side doors, Andy sat next to the driver.

The Papal Nuncio made the old cardinal very welcome to his beautiful home, personally escorted him to the VIP stateroom, then retired to his own office to make some frantic phone calls, some to the Prime Minister's office and some to Rome. He needed advice; he wasn't sure whether he was giving refuge to a criminal, a fraudster or… just perhaps… a hero!

Andrei was given an office he could use, and very soon the journalist was making financial arrangements with the main British newspapers; then the Australian newspapers.

It was from the Sydney journalists that Andrei discovered the full story of *what* the Cardinal had been doing, when he had that disastrous accident which led to him being declared 'dead'.

He read with glee about the Requiem Mass offered for the soul of the man thought to be dead! *With an empty coffin*! Oh Boy! he had so much material he didn't know where to start.

He couldn't believe his luck! He listened intently, made copious notes, informed the British newspapers he had a scoop for them, haggled strenuously over the fee and sent off, there and then, all the details he had discovered.

The Papal Nuncio, aware of what the journalist was doing, advised Andrei to ask for a journalist named Bruce Wallis; he was a fine young man and, more importantly, he was a staunch defender of the Prime Minister.

Andrei and Bruce got on well and they agreed to share the glories equally. Bruce informed the Romanian that *his* newspaper was the one chosen by their gracious sovereign. In this way, the whole story of Charles, the Cardinal, would reach right up to the Palace itself. Andrei was thrilled.

The two men typed their stories until midnight, and thus the whole history of the Australian Cardinal was the top story, in all its splendour, on the front page of the morning editions the next day. The story even mentioned his off-beat activities such as having a camel as a pet, smuggling it into his country, blowing up the Retirement home and teaching the men to roller skate.

It finished with the cardinal's efforts to change a river's course in order to manufacture their own electricity and very nearly killed himself and, in that particular project, his pet, Gertrude, was drowned trying to save him.

* * *

Meanwhile, at Downing Street. The Prime Minister glanced at the clock; it was nearly 2.00am.

"Robert, Robert, come here quickly", called the PM urgently. Her confidential secretary came running.

"PM?" answered the weary young man.

"See if you can get me Bruce Wallis on the phone. He might still be awake and active."

"Shall do, PM, as fast as I can". Robert hurried away, thinking – but unable to say so – there would be no sensible person awake at the ridiculous hour of two in the morning, and be still working – except him!

However, he was wrong. Bruce was yawning widely, but was nearly finished his work, and was looking forward to his bed with a vengeance.

The confidential line buzzed, and he swore softly as he reached for the wretched thing.

"Bruce Wallis speaking…Who? …I beg your pardon! … Goodness gracious! Forgive me, Prime Minister, I answered so rudely. I didn't know…"

"Bruce, this is a dreadful time to call anybody, especially one who works as hard as you do. Please forgive me, but I couldn't leave my office without expressing my heart-felt gratitude for the magnificent coverage you manage to get of the visit to St Bede's hospital this afternoon and the really flattering account of our donation of one million pounds to that excellent establishment…"

"That is exceedingly kind of you Prime Minister…there was no need…"

"Indeed, there was, Bruce. The photo-shoot alone of me handing over the cheque was simply superb; thank you also for the ones of me with both Dr Wangchi – excellent young man that he is – his fiancé, and the photo of me with the good doctor's parents. They are beautiful people."

"Indeed, they are delightful people. But, Prime Minister, it is I who should have been calling you, for letting me in on that visit today to St Bede's. It gave me the chance to meet Dr Wangchi and the chance to talk with him. This has led to him asking me to write a series of articles on his experiences, and the medical improvements he suggested should be installed in the prison system."

The PM was impressed. "That is marvellous. Bruce, tell me, does the good doctor harbour great resentment at our treatment of him by thrusting the poor chap into prison and misjudging him by, virtually, branding him a traitor, a spy?"

"Not at all, PM. He said, after the initial shock was over, and he had done all he could to protect his cards and passport, he looked on the time there as a real chance to see what prison life was actually like; any moneys lost were, apparently, immaterial to him.

"He said most of his patients at St Bede's came from prison, or had been in prison, so he had always wanted to see for himself, the hygiene, the food, the washing facilities, in fact, all that constitutes living behind bars. He was particularly interested in studying the psychological effects prison life would make on a reasonably normal human being." Bruce started to laugh.

"In fact, while he was there, he made copious notes and thought he would try to use the time spent there as a Tax Deduction, calling it 'work-directed-analysis', on his Returns this coming year" Bruce began to laugh again, and to his delight, the PM joined in." They chatted for a few more minutes, said good night and broke the connection.

The Prime Minister looked at Robert.

"I think, my boy, we've done it. If we can just pull off this Reception tomorrow, we're home and hosed, I think.

"Robert, I'm totally exhausted, and you must be even more so. Let's pack it in and get home for what's left of the night. We have to be bright and bubbly tomorrow and that's only a few hours away. Go quickly, my boy, or I'll think up something else I want you to do."

She laughed and waited until the young man had left the office, then turned off the light, buzzed for her car and was soon driven the short distance to No 10 Downing Street.

THE PRODIGAL GETS IT ALL

After it was over, the next ten days were a bewildering kind of blur to Charles.

*

As Charles, exhausted, lay back in his First-Class chair/bed on his way back home to Australia, his mind ranged over the extraordinary events that had occurred in the past week.

He thought with delight – mixed with a huge amount of relief – of his meeting with the young doctor whose clothes he had stolen. He had been perspiring freely as he waited, fully and regally dressed as a Prince of the Church, for the tall young man to come towards him at the Prime Minister's reception. He started to tremble and had a desperate desire to flee – to run like hell; he knew his whole future depended on this youngster. He could end up…he had shuddered slightly at the thought…in jail!

Dr Wangchi had held out his hand but, looking at the tall aristocratic man in front of him, he saw through the outward show, to the fear within, so taking both of the cardinal's hands, the young man moved forward and embraced him. Charles had been overwhelmed. The tears started falling and the young man had then kept whispering: "It's all right, sir, it's all right! Don't let them see you in tears."

Charles had wrapped his arms around the good doctor and held him tightly. Dr Wangchi had kept whispering that he understood the whole situation; he had treated many men who had lost any idea of who they were and had done extraordinary things… but, the young man started to laugh, happily…no one had done quite what Charles York had done!

Charles, who had a freaky sense of humour, had started to laugh helplessly, and the two of them – the stars in this show – had soon been seen laughing helplessly in front of the distinguished crowd of guests – to their astonishment.

Dr Wangchi had broken this up, by asking, if he could present his fiancé, Ms Elizabeth Travers whom he was hoping to marry very soon, then his mother and father, who were overwhelmed at the gracious and kindly reception by the cardinal.

All this had been captured on film by the clever Andrei and Bruce Wallis.

At the doctor's request, the cardinal was included in the Press photo of the medal presentation by the Prime Minister. The cardinal stood in the background with the doctor's parents who were smiling proudly.

It was then that the Prime Minister had taken Charles in hand and introduced him to the members of her Cabinet who were present, drinks were then handed around by servants, directed by Robert, and soon, there had been a happy, 'party' attitude pervading the whole room. The PM had stolen a secret look with Robert; both of them had smiled and sighed with relief – it seemed the crisis had been averted!

Gifts were exchanged, Charles, from the nuncio's private store of gifts, gave the young couple large, beautiful, pure silver, medals of St Thomas of Canterbury, in exquisite cases of tooled leather.

In return Dr Wangchi and his parents had given Charles a hand-painted, and written, treasure: a copy of a13th century original manuscript of the 'Book of the Hours'.

The old cardinal had gasped at the gift; it was truly magnificent – a treasure indeed! He showed it to the PM who, too, had been overwhelmed.

Soon, it was time to go and the PM had walked with the cardinal to the door of the Reception room. She had then leaned towards him at the door and whispered. Charles looked up, shocked out of his mind. "*Me*?" he had queried, his mouth falling open.

"Yes *you*, Your Eminence!" she had answered. "I'll be in touch tomorrow with the Nunciature to inform you of the time." She had then cast a quick look around, found herself unobserved, genuflected quickly and kissed his ring. "Goodbye, Your Eminence, you have nearly given me a nervous breakdown, but also an experience I'll never forget!"

She had hurried back to her guests with a glad heart.

Charles and the Nuncio had then returned to the Nunciature. It was there that Charles bewildered his host by informing him that he had been invited to the palace. The Nuncio had rushed to his chapel praying fervently that this guest, famous as he undoubtedly was, would go home soon.

In all his time in London he, the official representative of the Vatican in this country, had never before met so many of the illustrious rulers of the country and *he* had never been invited to the palace, not even once!

He had been heard muttering by his secretary: 'These bloomin' Colonials!'

* * *

The young air steward leant over Charles seeing him awake.

"Your Eminence, I notice you are not sleeping. Are you in any pain, or discomfort? Perhaps, I could get you a drink? It might put you to sleep."

"You're a good chap. Thank you. I would like a small whiskey; it might do the trick. But only if you have it and that it's no trouble."

The air steward laughed softly. "We certainly have it, Eminence. I'll only be a moment – it's a wonderful flight, so smooth and peaceful; it's a pity not to sleep; you'll have a lot to do when you face the Press tomorrow morning, I would think." The man went to move away when Charles stopped him.

"Would you tell me who is making that astonishing noise, snoring so loudly; I've never heard anything like it in my life before."

The Steward laughed gently. "That, Eminence, is the famous – or *once was famous*, forty years ago – rock singer, Roy 'The Boy' Morgue Stickelbacker. He's on his way to Australia for his very last concert. That's the 23rd last Concert he has a given, to my knowledge!"

"Can he still sing?"

"No, to be honest he can barely croak, but with masses of coloured flashing lights and coloured smoke bombs, screaming music from the band, people think he's great; I think he's the absolute pits myself".

Charles nodded, knowingly, but as soon as the man had gone to get the drink, Charles wondered about the 'pits'. What were they? Where were they? What did the good man mean? He forced himself to listen to the frightful snoring and decided, 'the pits' had to mean the snorer was hopeless.

Charles, always trying to be charitable, thought, well his snoring is in the top class at any rate.

He made up his mind to ignore the dreadful sound and, soon

he was sipping slowly a small glass of excellent whiskey while his mind flew to the palace and the gracious reigning sovereign lady herself.

THE SOVEREIGN TRUMPS THE DUKE

He remembered the briefing he had been given – the protocol he must use to greet the Sovereign. He needed it; it had been years since he had been in the crowd of VIPs to greet her whenever she had come to his country: How to stand; how to bow the head, how to address the monarch, to the extent that – with all this running around his head - when he had arrived at the reception room, waiting for the queen, he was totally confused as to what he was to do, or say.

One surprise had followed the other. First Charles had been astonished at the tiny figure that confronted him; she appeared to have shrunk half his size since he saw her last. He remembered to bow his head while standing straight as an arrow, frightened to death.

However, the small woman, used to thousands and thousands of awkward introductions, took over, and within minutes had the Cardinal chuckling, and at ease.

Charles had been charmed by the beautiful voice; so clearly pronounced, each syllable, so perfectly uttered. When his mind had clicked into what was being said, he received a shock. He'd had to ask her to repeat her statement.

The queen had smiled, and repeated. “Your Eminence, I’m going to kidnap you and we’re off to my private sitting room where Philip and I want to talk to you.”

Good Heavens, Charles had thought. I’m going to meet the Duke as well. He walked behind the monarch to her private ‘escape room’ – as she told Charles, she called it – wondering what on earth they were going to talk about. Philip had been in the Navy, he recalled; Charles hoped the conversation would not be anything about that; he knew nothing of naval matters, or anything about warfare.

In the beautiful, comfortable room, a Lady in Waiting was standing there with a number of shoe boxes. Charles had been bewildered to be asked – as soon as he had entered the room – his shoe size. He had mumbled: “Eleven, I think, Ma’am.” Apparently, that was all that was needed.

The small woman had gestured to the chairs. “Sit, sit, sit. Eminence. …Oh, dear! I’m sorry, you haven’t met Philip.” She took hold of her husband’s arm and brought him over to their visitor. Charles had begun to struggle out of his comfortable chair, only to be stopped by the queen.

“No, no! Stay there. You can meet the Duke from there.” The two men had shaken hands, Charles had remembered to mutter: ‘Your Royal Highness’ while noticing that the Duke waited for instructions from his wife. The queen gestured again to the chairs, and Philip sat down next to his wife – after she had seated herself first.

The queen had then looked fixedly at her visitor. She spoke crisply.

“Eminence, I don’t have to tell you what it is like to spend your entire life in the blaze of the cameras, the flashing of cameras everywhere you move; if you want to sneeze, you have to make sure no one is watching and even a simple little thing like walking through the shops is forbidden. A Press man might leap out at you just as you are examining, and possibly considering buying, some nice new dates flown in from Mexico, or some such place."

The small lady had smiled. "Forgive me, Eminence, I grow loquacious in my very old age" She had taken her husband's hand. "Poor Philip has had to be left behind me like a puppy following his master. But you know all that. You understand well, that you, in your position, are really in the same position as we are. There are so many things we have wanted to do and simply were not permitted to do." She had begun to smile broadly as she continued.

"And, one of the things we really have always wanted to do was to learn to roller skate." Charles had begun to perspire with dread of the next question, as he knew quite well what it was going to be. He'd tried to get in first.

"No, no, no, no! I couldn't take the responsibility Ma'am." He had stuttered in a hoarse voice.

"There's no responsibility, Eminence," the queen had declared firmly. "That is the reason, Lady Anne, is here. My senior Lady in waiting is to shoulder all the responsibility for permitting me to foolishly roller skate with you, in this very room. She has pledged her word… on the condition you teach her as well!"

The queen, Philip and Lady Anne had all laughed happily.

The Duke had leaned forward. "Well, what about it, old chap? Will you take on three amateurs? It would be great delight for us – and a break from the ordinary round of dreary engagements."

Charles had realised he had no option. He'd tried to make it clear he was no expert; he had only skated a few times himself. He had finally stood up; he'd made a decision. Whether it was right or wrong, and whatever the conclusion, he was going to do it!

He had looked around the very large room. Yes, he'd thought

there was room enough; there was a good long space down one side of the room and if a couple of chairs could be moved, he could make it a circular track.

He moved quickly, shifting the chairs himself, effortlessly. He'd then informed the three pupils to put on their skates and to give him a pair to wear. Lady Anne hastened to obey and, with a bit of shuffling all four of them were soon booted and ready for action.

Charles had been relieved to see the skates were the same as he had used at the Retirement Home –the ones with the little brake at the toe end.

Charles demonstrated how to stand up, pushing the brake into the floor and was relieved to see they followed instructions closely. He then had emphasized the need to bend far forward, pressing their weight down into the floor so they wouldn't fall backwards. This accomplished, he bowed to the queen and ask if he might take her hand. She smiled and extended her hand. He held it tightly and advising her as they went, slowly – very – slowly, down the passage between the furniture.

Lady Anne came next and quickly picked up the basic points and took the queen's hand while he had then attempted to teach the Duke. He'd found Philip had a tendency to bolt like a horse; it had taken all of Charles' strength to hold him steady. Philip had a distinct leaning to the left and a superlative, huge antique bowl in brilliant colours, standing on a column at shoulder height, seemed to attract him, as he bumped into it each time they went down that way.

To Charles' surprise the queen had a natural sense of rhythm, so he'd begun to sing to the 'Skater' Waltz' – as it had no words he used 'la, da, la da' and was delighted to hear the queen's sweet, clear voice singing with him. Lady Anne soon joined in and then had come the Duke, who had no sense of tune, or rhythm at all – he had a voice like a bull.

The women had then wanted to go alone and they did, one at a time. Charles had been frightened of letting the Duke go alone, and held on grimly to his hand, as Philip lurched, rather than glided down the aisle.

Soon the monarch and lady Anne were doing the entire circuit with ease and with intense enjoyment. Charles had been thrilled to see that it had been a success – at least with the women. He could not see that Philip would ever have the balance and rhythm needed. He had continued to hold the Duke's hand until he had been shaken off, irritably, and been told, brusquely, he was going alone, so 'to let go of him' – which Charles had to do.

Philip had set off at a pace that had frightened Charles. He called a warning; Elizabeth seeing the danger added her voice, while Lady Anne called out loudly, "Be careful! You're heading straight for the..."

There had been an ear-splitting smashing-sound as Philip had crashed into the antique vase, knocking it, the pedestal...and himself, as well, to the floor.

And, not only just knocked the vase to the floor! Charles found, to his horror, that the Duke was sitting there on the floor uttering echoing groans and yells through the hole at the top of the vase. His head appeared to be stuck in the vase which was now where his head should have been.

Charles had rushed to rescue the man. The women came as fast as they could. What to do? The vase seemed to be tightly jammed onto the Duke's head.

The queen had moved first. "Eminence, see if we can lift it off." The two of them, tugging from each side, had not been able to move it an inch. Philip had yelled louder, with each pull they made, and said many expletives that would have been appropriate for the time he had been captain in a submarine, but definitely, not in this setting: Charles had pretended he didn't hear them.

The queen was perplexed and had moved backward, forgetting she was on skates and went for a tumble, fortunately onto a couch, while poor Lady Anne came down with a loud bump, in an unladylike manner, ending up sprawled on her back on the floor. Charles had rushed to the rescue and helped the embarrassed woman to her feet.

The Queen had then ordered them to get rid of the skates quickly as someone could come in at any minute. Elizabeth then removed Philip's. Then, in their own shoes they'd gathered around Philip who was emitting load groans from inside the vase.

Charles had then seen Lady Anne, whispering to Elizabeth, then bundle all the skates she could see, including Charles', into a box out of sight. Then to Charles' astonished eyes, he had seen Elizabeth advancing on the vase with a wooden croquet mallet which had been in the cupboard.

Charles had expressed his worries, that if the queen smashed the vase with a wooden mallet, what could happen to Philip's head *inside* the vase? Elizabeth told him, crisply, not to be a 'fuss pot', and taking aim smashed the vase to pieces and released a very relieved, red-faced man, whose eyes appeared to be crossed! His wife had then given him a very vigorous shake, and told to 'pull yourself together', which seemed to do the trick.

Charles had hoisted the stricken man to his feet, thanking God that Philip was apparently unharmed by the accident. In fact, he had begun to laugh as he spoke to Charles, rubbing his head with one of his hands.

"You see, Eminence," Philip had whispered, "everyone thinks Elizabeth is a sweet little, fragile woman; they couldn't be further from the truth. She's a ruthless tough old biddy who belts her poor old hubby up!" He'd laughed loudly.

"You can see why I walk behind her; I'm too frightened to

walk in front." He had then leaned across and kissed his wife, who had simply laughed and shook her fist at him.

Charles and Lady Anne laughed with them. Charles had then remembered the mess of the broken vase. "Should we attempt to clean up this mess?" Elizabeth had shaken her head; she'd smiled as she replied:

"Definitely not, Eminence. First, we must set the scene. First the props." Charles had watched, entranced, as the two women set up what looked like afternoon tea and told them where to sit in a small circle where two couches faced one another. Then Elizabeth had given instructions to Anne: "Bring in the corgis."

A door had opened and soon three little corgis were scampering around their mistress. Elizabeth had then given an order and the three dogs settled at her feet. She nodded to Lady Anne who went to a bell cord and rang the bell.

A house servant had appeared almost immediately. The queen had raised her eyes from her guest and had spoken quickly and firmly. "An accident. I shouldn't have had the dogs here…foolish of me! Please attend to it." She turned her head to their guest. "And, Eminence, you were telling me about your wonderful land, so sunny, so many wonderful beaches, so much space. I love your country and visited it as often as I could get away with it." She had laughed gently; the others had laughed with her.

At that moment both Charles and Elizabeth noticed that one of the Duke's skates had been overlooked and was sticking out from under a cushion. Charles had risen to the occasion, literally. He'd stood up, naturally, and moved to sit with the cushion at his back.

"I'm sorry, please excuse me, Ma'am…bad back…need something straight now to sit comfortably…all the ceremonies, you know how it is. I truly don't know how you do it."

Elizabeth quickly had taken up the life-line that Charles had given her: “I agree, totally, Your Eminence. I, too, find it now extremely difficult to do, yet it is expected I do it. It was easy in the beginning with the wonderful training my sister Margaret and I had received from our grandmother, Queen Mary. She demanded we sit and stand with straight backs from three years onwards.”

“Indeed?”

“Strangely, Eminence, I don’t have any trouble when riding; I never even feel inclined to slump; it’s only when I’m opening Parliament and listening to other people’s speeches that my back seems to want to give way.” Charles had laughed, realising the little, secret, joke the queen was making.

By this time the cleaners had come and gone and with them had gone, also, the priceless Etruscan vase. When the door closed, the tea-party sham was over. The queen stood up. Her guests did likewise.

Elizabeth came forward with her hand out while Lady Anne rang another bell for the Butler.

It was then the Royals had said their goodbyes. Elizabeth held the cardinal’s hand tightly.

“Your Eminence, this is the third time we’ve met, if I remember correctly. Each time Philip and I have visited your beautiful country, you were in the VIP group to receive us.

“However, each of those times we were all on ‘duty’. We were stiff and formal. This visit, to us, is such a contrast. Here I have felt that you were a guest in my home and someone who felt at home with us. That is precious to us. It was a tremendous risk I was taking, in asking you to come and teach us to skate. But it worked! I had a wonderful afternoon and, when the Duke gets over his headache, and the black eye begins to fade, he’ll think the same.

“Goodbye and God bless you, Eminence. It has been a joy to see you again. Thank God for that journalist who wrote all the details about you; after reading all that I knew you would enter into our little interlude of nonsense gladly, and I was right…t…… ttttttt……."

Charles turned over and mumbled, "… and, I was right…t." The Air Steward looked at his passenger and saw he was now settled; he was dead to the world. With infinite care, he turned out the bed light and moved silently away.

CLERICAL CONFUSION CAUSES CHAOS

The Archbishop Samuel Spotels was dithering in his excitement. For the fourth time, he asked the VG if it were time to leave, to welcome the old Cardinal home.

Fr Jack Okiama sighed. "Your Grace, you know very well, we can't leave for another thirty minutes. Please relax. Sit down, and tell me what you plan to do, with our globe-trotting elderly reverend gentleman."

Sammy sat down, but declared they would leave early; he couldn't just sit around; he was too tense. He then remembered the VG had asked him a question.

"Jack, I don't really know. I want to hug him and kick him at the same time. He has caused us all so much trouble, and grief, and look what he's done to those good Sisters." He removed his zucchetto and scratched his head. "However, he must be ninety by now, surely. Perhaps he might give up his desire for a riotous lifestyle and just settle down…"

The VG broke in.

"Your Grace, don't forget Vera Lynn released an album for her 100th birthday, didn't she?"

"Thank you, VG for those cheering words. And, with that we're off. Come on, I can't bear the suspense any longer."

CHARLES MAKES HIS STAGE DEBUT

When the three clerics arrived at the airport, they were astonished at the size of the crowd that was waiting for the flight. There seemed to be thousands assembled there, while police were everywhere, trying to control this mob of people.

"What the hell's going on?" demanded Sammy. "Is a famous politician coming in on this flight, or something? This can't be for the cardinal!" The VG whispered that he had just seen a policeman he knew, so he'd go and see what he could find out.

Father Jack Okiama was only away a few minutes. When he returned to Sammy, he told them his news, speaking softly.

"There's a famous old rock-singer, a Roy 'The Boy' Morgue Stickelbacker, arriving, and he's going to perform one of his hits here, at the airport, before he's whizzed off elsewhere."

The Archbishop grunted. "Never heard of him. Have you two?"

"My mother was a fan once," confessed Monsignor Izzy Grim. "Long before my time. He's well and truly an old wreck now."

Sammy was irritated. "Why do these old 'has-beens' always seem to do one of their very last concerts in Australia? We must be very stupid, or tone deaf. Look at the crowd he's collected... Look out!" he suddenly shouted, excitedly: "The plane's landed!"

* * *

The three clerics surged forward through the huge crowd of people.

Messages were pouring out of the loudspeaker system but also from the megaphones of the frenetic crowd, screaming in anticipation of the arrival of their hero; 'Roy the Boy'.

Sammy tried to listen to the directions, being offered to the crowd, but gave it up; it was simply impossible to understand. The three clerics pushed on until they found themselves almost fronting a hastily assembled platform, or stage. It was then they realised they had come to the wrong place.

They turned intending to retrace their steps, but in vain. They were blocked. Sammy was starting to go a dangerous 'rose' colour. Izzy and Jack moved to warn him, when the attention of everyone, including the three men, was focused on a blasting ear-splitting scream of fans as a Fan fare of trumpets ushered onto the stage a bewildered elderly cardinal, blinking in the blaze of lights.

Sammy, Jack and Izzy stared with their mouths open. Nothing had prepared them for this! The crowd didn't know what to make of the situation, then one young man shouted; 'He's dressed up! Come, on, give us your favourite, 'Kill me Baby!' The band started up with enormous volume, the lights were flashing, and two of the coloured smoke bombs were let off.

Charles, up there on the stage, was the first to really grasp what had happened. He stood perfectly still and began to sing. The band faltered. What the hell was he singing… or, trying to sing?

There was a sudden deafening silence in the crowd. They listened. At last they heard the old, strong voice of the Cardinal, as he intoned the Kyrie!

"Ky-ri-e…e-le-i-son…Chri-ste...ei…son."

...That was as far as he got before the tomato hit him smack on the chin and the screams of rage began. Missiles began to come thick and fast after that.

Soon the stage was littered with food, rubbish of all kinds; Charles was soon a dripping, wet, mess. Then he straightened up. He wasn't going to put up with this! He looked around for weapons and seized one of the band pieces – the musicians had fled.

He started to sing again, loudly this time,

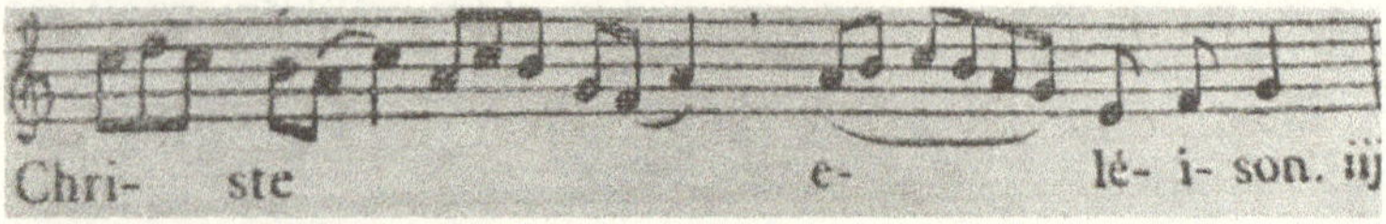

"Chri...ste......e...le..i..son...

Take that, you bovine ass!" A drum went next. Then two music stands went flying from the stage, "*Oh, you would*, would you! Take that!" Another drum went sailing through the air – it was the bass drum. It was expertly thrown and encircled the protesting youth knocking him to the ground, with the drum around his hips and his mouth open, gasping, until he went still... His supporters screeched, shouting:

"Murderer! Murderer! Murderer!" Charles continued singing as he shouted: "Take that, you might learn to read, you ignorant, baboon!" A heavy, leather, carry-bag of music, went sailing across the crowd knocking two more young men to the floor. "*le...i... son...* Ugh!" Charles had been hit with a messy meat pie half eaten.

Sammy saw, to his dismay, the old man, in his fury, throw another drum through the air, and knock three young men to the floor. They were screaming, in anger, or in pain, he wasn't sure which. A Cymbal sliced through the air next, while music stands, and microphones, seemed to be hitting their targets with stunning accuracy.

The cardinal was starting to enjoy himself.

Sammy realised he had to do something. "Come on, fellas, it's up to us, now!" So, saying, Sammy hitched up his cassock, closed his fists and surged forward to defend the old man.

All three men were in fine physical condition: Sammy had continued his routine that he had always followed and took keeping fit very seriously. Monsignor Isidore Grim's father had made sure his son knew how to defend himself when he was at secondary school, and was a fairly good, bare-knuckled, fist fighter, while Jack Okiama's Japanese father had made sure his son had a good grounding in kickboxing and in all the martial arts, using the side of the hands.

In all, the three were a formidable trio.

The three rescuers ploughed head-first into the mob, punching, hitting and slicing their way to the stage leaving, literally, at least a dozen young men, lying helplessly in the aisle, yelling their heads off at 'clerical brutality'. It wasn't all one-sided. Sammy was now wearing a badly bruised eye from a direct heavy punch – which to his humiliation – was delivered by a hefty woman, while the Monsignor had a bloody nose, but Jack seemed to have escaped any obvious scars.

The police looked on with admiration, just sorry they were prevented from using the same techniques!

Charles saw Sammy fighting his way towards him and bellowed: "Sammy, save me!".

Sammy was the first to climb onto the stage, grab the cardinal and half drag, half carry, the old man back through the exit from which he had entered. Izzy and Jack worked as a back-up team, leaving the stage backwards, and fighting to the very end.

As the last of the three passed the exit door, it was slammed shut and all four men, leant against the walls of, what turned out to be the VIP departure lounge. They stayed there for a moment or two to catch their breaths and consider the situation they had created.

"You realise, Izzy and Jack, that the blasted TV cameras were covering the entire proceedings? We'll be on TV news to-night, you can bet your bottom dollar." He gently patted his left eye. "Tell me, quickly, how bad is this eye? Will it be a dreadful shiner?" The two young clerics examined the eye critically.

"I'm sorry, Your Grace, it's going to be a beauty," declared Izzy. "You'll be recognized everywhere you go by the eye. You copped a frightful one there".

"Oh, hell! But what about yourself, Izzy, there's blood coming from your nose, and Jack, you're limping? Are you both all right?"

The Monsignor declared the nosebleed was nothing; it would stop in a minute or two, but Jack said he needed some massage, he thought, he could have pulled a muscle – he hadn't kick-boxed for some time. He declared his muscles had grown flabby; he must practise more. As always, he had a quip to add: "I didn't realise that priestly life could be so entertaining, and so *energetic*!"

Sammy was relieved, although all were 'wounded', nothing was too serious. Now, for the cardinal; he was reluctant to even turn to face him. He forced himself to turn around.

The cardinal was crying.

"Oh, Sammy!" the old man cried, "I been looking forward to this moment for so long and …now *THIS*! Sammy… *I never intended…*" He rushed forward and buried his head in Sammy's arms.

Sammy grinned. "Eminence, I think we'll write those famous words on your coffin as the 'leitmotiv' of your life. But, first remind me to dig up your coffin; we'll use that one, it's empty; I'm all for saving when we can…."

The Archbishop was interrupted by the Police Chief Inspector.

"Gentlemen, I'm terribly sorry. It's all our fault, not yours, or the Cardinal's." Sammy looked surprised.

"How is that, sir? I've been blaming the cardinal for all the mess…"

"We goofed up! That's the long and the short of it. We had two celebrities coming on that plane: the cardinal here and an old, but very famous Rock Singer – 'old' is the word, sir; he was the rage when I was young; I'm now sixty. However, that's as may be, but we were supposed to put the cardinal into a small private lounge and the pop singer in here. We found the small lounge had been previously booked by a small group of elderly women who were seeing a member of their group off on a holiday. The police Inspector on duty thought he could solve the situation by shunting the cardinal into the larger area, while he put the singer into the Ladies' group lounge."

"*What*? You must be joking! Has your man been smoking something, Chief Inspector?" Sammy was hotly indignant at such a ludicrous arrangement, but then, his sense of the ridiculous asserted himself, and he and the two young priests, began to laugh helplessly.

"And, pray tell, how is the rock singer, doing in the old ladies' lounge?"

The policeman began to laugh.

"I don't honestly know. but first we must finish this fiasco. It was all our fault and you were simply defending this elderly gentleman – that part is clear. However, several people have been slightly injured and will be seeking to sue, not only your party, but the Police Force, the Airport officials and, God alone knows who else.

"I've contacted my superiors, and they are aghast at such a debacle. They suggested I take a statement from each of you, including the cardinal, then we'll try to get an appearance before a Magistrate tomorrow morning and he, with the Commissioner behind him, will declare a natural mistake had been made, due to overwhelming tension and inadequate senior police available to cope with the situation, with no malice, or infringement of Religious, or Age Discrimination, or any other laws, involved.

"The management here – who naturally are only too anxious to assist – have provided an office where we could go now and get the statements over and done with. Then you can take the old gentleman home but, just remember you have to be at the Magistrate's Court tomorrow morning."

The policeman sighed wearily. "Does that sound OK with you, Archbishop?"

"It sounds fine, Sir. We'll do the statements now, as you suggest, and, don't worry, we'll all be there at the Court tomorrow morning." The Chief Inspector smiled and shook hands with all the clerics, including the old cardinal. He held the hand of the cardinal.

"You wouldn't know, sir, but I was one of the policemen who declared you dead when we saw you briefly as you were being washed away in the flood. When I saw you on the TV, in London with the Prime Minister, I said to the wife: '*If ever I did see, a dead man it was he*'. You've surprised all of us, sir and I, for one, am mighty glad I was wrong!"

Sammy rounded up his group. "Come on lads, and you too, Eminence; we're off home and then, His Eminence will tell us just how he escaped death, flew all round the world, visited the Palace and, eventually, decided to return home – the old villain that he really is!"

ROY 'THE BOY' CANCELS HIS TOUR

In the small private lounge, Mrs Ethel Rutledge, the president of the 'Exhilarated Eighties' was aghast; she looked at the singer they had hired with unbelief.

The members of the ladies' group were similarly dismayed. Two members lost their false eyelashes in their shock, while three who had been under the knife for face-lifts, were outraged to discover that, with the tightening of their skin, they were unable, visually, to express their outrage! Their tongues, however, were unaffected.

Was it some kind of joke they wondered?

With the first blast of his voice, poor Roy Morgue, as he tried to sing without his band, the flashing lights, and the coloured smoke bombs, only managed to get out a loud, disastrous, piercing, screaming sound.

Mrs Rutledge had to turn her hearing aid off. Her head was ringing with the pain the noise had caused.

She noticed that Nancy, who was soon to board her plane, was looking quite ill and her top denture had fallen out. Ethel decided, as president, she simply had to do something about it. She clapped her hands to get the singer's attention, turned her hearing aid back on, and spoke kindly, but sharply.

"I'm, sure, sir that the song you just rendered would be very pleasing to others, when your throat has recovered from whatever it is you are suffering from. However, as we have paid for a performer, and you have turned up, you can now earn your money and sing some of our old favourites.

"You could start with some of Vera Lynn's songs; they are all so well known to us." She turned to the small group of members.

"What about, '*We'll meet again*', girls? It's suitable for we'll definitely be seeing Nancy again, after her wonderful trip, and then she can tell us of all the great sights she has seen and all the wonderful people she has met." Ethel Rutledge then, turning to the singer, instructed him, brusquely.

"'*We'll meet again*', thank you." There was silence. Ethel hissed: "Get on with it, idiot!"

Roy Morgue Stickelbaker, turned a dreadful shade of grey; his eyes rolled up and he fainted.

Mrs Rutledge was furious. She rang the bell immediately and demanded they remove the prostrate form as quickly as possible; he was ruining their farewell party. Heads will roll, she warned, if they dare send them anyone as bad as that one was, ever again.

Ethel was determined nothing was going to spoil their party, so made herself the leader and chose the songs they loved.

Soon, they were singing their hearts out, having forgotten entirely poor Roy Morgue who, recovering in the emergency department of the city hospital, made arrangements with his agent on his phone, to fly back to the US, by the night flight.

He would never, he determined, attempt to try the Australian audiences ever again: they were too fickle.

AN OPERATIC TRAGEDY, WORTHY OF VERDI

Meanwhile, John and his wife Diane Foggarty, were preparing to enter the large hall, being directed there by a very confused airport official. They had been engaged by a Mrs Ethel Rutledge

Both performers were making last minute checks, in their mirrors, on their appearance, before they entered. Having sung in the Opera Chorus for many years, they now took on gigs, such as this one, for the old folks, to sing the songs they loved singing, and to let people who liked good music, be entertained. They were good people with beautiful voices.

They had decided to do a series of Nelson Eddy and Jeanette McDonald duets, starting with the famous song: '*The Indian Love Call*' from the musical, '*Rose Marie*' which had been made into a film. Diane had suggested to John that he walk on first, singing and looking, not at the audience, but at the entrance, from whence would come, his beloved. The side curtain would then open and reveal the pianist at the piano, as Diane appeared.

That, at least, had been the plan.

Poor John Foggarty walked onto the large stage, singing his heart out to a huge group of disappointed and very, angry people. They had been deprived of their great hero, Roy 'The Boy'

Morgue; they then had to endure some religious nut; and *NOW, to be given THIS!*

The crowd was furious! John got no further than the first half of one line before the barrage began. He screamed in terror, as bottles came crashing all around him. Diane rushed out to see what was happening; she copped a bag of flour in her face and nearly choked. When she was able to do so, she screamed at the top of her coloratura range, for help. Police rushed in from every entrance.

It was a nightmare! They had to call an ambulance for what was left of poor John and Diane.

Not knowing what had happened, Mr and Mrs Foggarty determined that was the end of their entertaining 'old folks'!

The elderly were far too dangerous!

THE SOVEREIGN RELAXES

The queen walked wearily from her car to her private apartment. As she entered her rooms, the corgis burst into happy yapping. Elizabeth greeted them and stood still, as Lady Anne took the hat and gloves of her Lady. Elizabeth then spoke to her husband.

"Please Philip, no foolish talk this evening. I'm very tired. You watch the TV news, record it, and then you can tell me later – when Lady Anne brings me a cup of tea – whether there is anything I need to know." She sat in a deep cushioned chair, closed her eyes and relaxed her muscles as she leaned back gratefully. She was suddenly aware of Lady Anne removing her lace-up tight shoes and putting her feet into big fluffy slippers.

She smiled her relief and her gratitude. "You certainly can read me like a book, Lady Anne. Thank you, one thousand times. That feels like heaven."

"Well, Ma'am, I know your schedule today; you've been on your feet for five hours straight. If you weren't tired… dare I say, '*dead beat*' – as my rough and tough brother says – you wouldn't be human. Just sit there for a moment, I'll get the tea."

Elizabeth now relaxed, turned to Philip. "What one earth are you chuckling about, dear? If it's politicians, I don't want to know! I've been with them for hours and I don't think I could cope with even hearing about them at the moment – unless I have to, of course."

Philip laughed outright. "I think dear, you'll find this, not only funny but interesting. It's mainly about a recent friend of ours who visited us here."

"Not …not…the old …cardinal?"

"The very same, love. Wait, I'll turn the machine around and wind it back to the part I want."

As soon as the queen saw the airport, she said: "That's Sydney, Australia, isn't it? And…Philip, you know I hate rock singers and mobs of people. What are you showing me this for? ...Good Grief! …Is that our '*skating* cardinal'? What's he doing at a Rock Concert?"

"Just watch, he didn't actually intend to be there, love. Now, be quiet and watch the whole coverage."

Elizabeth sat up and watched with apprehension, then amusement, then outright laughter, the antics of the old man on the stage; then with consternation that he would be killed, then with relief and admiration at the antics of the three younger clerics, as they rescued the old man.

Lady Anne, standing behind the couch, watched with the queen and Philip; her laughter rang out with theirs.

Elizabeth turned to her husband. "Philip, you've made me forgot the horrid day I've had; I feel rejuvenated already. Come on, Lady Anne, pour the tea."

* * *

When all the formalities were over, the VG, Father Jack Okiama, drove the clerical party back to the Bishop's House. Back home, Sammy rang a doctor-friend of his and asked him to pop in, if he could do so, also a nurse he knew from the city hospital, to come and patch them up, if she too, was available.

Both doctor and nurse arrived together and went to work on the wounded. There was a fair amount of Betadine used, ice packs from the fridge were put on Sammy's eye but he was warned it would take days for the marks to disappear, while the VG's muscles got a work out with the fairly tough nurse, who was a whiz at sport injuries, and knew a lot about massaging torn and aching muscles.

Jack yelled a bit at some of her work, but had to admit, when it was over, she certainly knew her job; he was miles better than he had been.

Sammy, with his ice pack taped over his eye, directed the Cardinal to the showers and told him to dress in his pyjamas for he was going to bed as soon as they had eaten. All the men began to clean themselves up again and when all that was done, they ate a quiet meal, Charles in his dressing gown. Each man was trying to recover from the shock of the surprise they had encountered at the airport.

Meal finished, Sammy handed round a small glass of whiskey, then ordered the Cardinal to sit down and explain just what had happened to him; to give a good reason why he wasn't dead, when they had offered a Solemn Requiem for him and declared him dead! The very nerve of him!

Then, he told the old man, they all wanted to know, who the hell was this Dr Wangchi whose name he had been using, as he flew around the world – after stealing all his clothes.

Izzy, Jack and the old cardinal, all burst out laughing, then, with an effort Charles began his tale.

"You won't believe this, but this is what happened: I remember clearly the Bulldozer – it wasn't difficult to drive at all – I remember facing the high bank of the river…….."

When Charles' recital came to an end. Sammy glanced swiftly at his watch and said they should watch the Television news, briefly, to see if they had appeared during that dreadful 'welcoming' episode.

THE PUNCH-DRUNK PRELATE

Sammy thought they would be on the News but was hoping desperately that they would not.

It was the first story.

In all, it was a fairly accurate account of what had happened; the Television Station had obviously cleared it with the police, for the same Police Official, who had spoken to the clerics at the airport, declared, unequivocally, it had been their fault, not the clergy.

However, Sammy gritted his teeth as he heard himself called a 'Punch Drunk Prelate' and gave his background as the undisputed boxing champion of Oxford University.

The commentary joked that 'sinners had better beware of going to Confession to this priest; they could well be in mortal danger' and then proceeded to show a close-up of poor Sammy's face with his cut and bruised eye. He looked terrible: a disreputable drunken reprobate.

This was followed by an interview with the woman who gave the Archbishop the black eye. She was hailed as a 'hero for the cause'. When asked which cause did she espouse, she seemed a little vague and muttered something about 'ants being trodden on; they were a sacred species' – which didn't make a lot of sense, even to the reporter – who had once been bitten by a bull-ant – so he ended the interview.

The News Reader then went on to other news and Sammy, gratefully, switched the set off and turned to his companions.

"Well, now you know who you're dealing with. So, as a punch-drunk prelate, I'm ordering the lot of you to get to bed; we've had quite enough excitement for one day."

The men laughed and Sammy took the old Cardinal, now very weary, to his quarters; the old man was nearly out on his feet.

THE RETURN HOME OF THE DEAD MAN

At Mount St Francs' Retirement Home for Priests, the Superior, Mother Mary Angelica held a special meeting with both the Sisters, and the old priest residents, to discuss the welcome they should give to their globe-trotting escapee, Charles Cardinal York.

When everyone was seated, the Mother Superior spoke seriously to the group. "Now, I'm well aware that many of you, and our Sisters as well, want to do something to welcome back our truant Cardinal – the old devil." The assembly laughed.

"However, I've been speaking to the Archbishop and – I must admit I was surprised – but, it appears that His Eminence wants a very low-key return home. He is greatly fatigued, and after all his globe-trotting, he just wants to return quietly – without any fuss and just rest for the next few days. He has expressed his longing to be permitted just to wander about and see the vegetable gardens, the cattle, our Brothers' birds and, in general, quietly to see all the sights he has missed so greatly during the weeks he has been away." She noticed the disappointment on the faces looking at her.

"I do understand your disappointment, but – I know it's hard – try to remember, His Eminence is an old man; he has had been under extraordinary pressure and has even been to the Palace of the Queen in London.

"He has been headline news in just about every English Newspaper in the world, and has even been to receptions with the Prime Minister of England; sought by the Security Agencies of several countries, hunted as a possible traitor and spy, and for a good period of time, he thought he was actually Chinese." She smiled at the residents and Sisters.

"Truly, when you read of where he's been, and what he has done, it's enough to exhaust you, just reading about it. It's no wonder that the poor man just wants some peace and quiet.

"Now, I'm relying on you, gentlemen, and you, my Sisters, just to give the man a break for a couple of weeks. I'm sure, after that, His Eminence will be wanting so much to talk about his experiences that he'll drive us mad with them." She laughed and the men joined her.

"What I've decided, after discussions with the Sisters, is this. We welcome him quietly, we serve a special dinner and we let him wander, on his own to renew his acquaintance with all he loved at this beautiful place. If I think things are going well, I'll give him the gift you suggested I buy for him, straight after the dinner is completed, or if that's not suitable, I'll wait for the next day.

"If he asks for company to go with him on his walks, be ready to do so; otherwise, just let him be. Knowing, His Eminence, I don't think we'll have to wait long: he's a very gregarious man." She looked searchingly at the assembly. "All right?"

They nodded their agreement and the meeting broke up.

* * *

Father Jack Okiama drove Charles back to the Retirement Home three days after he had landed. When the car stopped, Mother

Superior stood waiting for him, Charles began to weep, softly. He hurried forward and pulled her up as she began to genuflect, to kiss his ring. "No, not after all the trouble I've caused. Please, Mother, don't."

"Oh, don't be such an idiot, Eminence! We were devastated at the thought of what had happened to you. This place is just bricks and mortar; you were our shining star; with you gone, the star had gone out." Angelica knew she had to be brisk now, otherwise she might just burst into tears herself, so she reverted to her usual manner with Charles.

"Now, get yourselves, organized, Eminence, we can't be standing out here 'yakking' away. The men are waiting for their dinner, if you're good, we might stretch a point and invite Fr Okiama to join us. We're looking forward to his conversation; it will be quite a change for us to have someone interesting to visit us for a change."

She turned to Jack Okiama, shook his hand vigorously and led him away, leaving Charles to walk behind on his own.

Angelica's treatment certainly put an end to Charles' self-pity. He looked in astonishment as Angelica linked her arm with Fr Okiama. The nerve of her! he muttered to himself. She hasn't changed a bit!

He picked up two of his cases, himself, and trudged behind, disgruntled.

* * *

The Archbishop Samuel Spotels waited impatiently for his VG to return from the Retirement Home.

He was worried about Charles. He seemed to have lost all his energy, his zest for living, his… 'Damn it!' Sammy thought angrily, 'he's become old!'

Ever since Sammy had first met the cardinal, he seemed to have an adolescent, bubbly, funny, 'Peter Pan' quality. He'd never seemed to be anything near his age. Now…?

Sammy was no longer sure about Charles. He did not know the serious, elderly, prelate he had become. Perhaps, he really is approaching his end. If that were so, Sammy didn't know how he would be able to cope with all that again. He had gone through all that, with the solemn Requiem, for the '*then believed dead*', cardinal.

Sammy was aware that his secretary, Monsignor Isidore Grim was waiting for him. He looked up with a start. "Sorry, Izzy, my mind is skittering all over the place. would you please read back a paragraph of those new instructions from Rome to me …"

CHARLES IS BACK!

The Archbishop needn't have worried about Charles. Even though Mother Angelica had advised extreme down-playing for the Cardinal's return, she couldn't hold back the roar of welcome that surged through the dining room when she led in the old man.

Charles beamed. The men had not forgotten him, nor do they hold grudges against him for nearly drowning them, when he had caused the river to break its banks and they'd been submerged.

Carefully watching the Cardinal, Angelica, led him to each of the tables and he shook hands with all the priests present. He even hugged his special friends, Belcher, Stinko, and Ted in his wheelchair. He then went to his own table which had been kept bare out of respect.

Sister Margaret came out from the kitchen, genuflected, kissed the cardinal's ring then returned to her work. A few of the other Sisters, including Paul, Veronica and Bernard, who were distributing the food in the dining room, welcomed him back quietly and happily.

The meal proceeded with music softly playing and it was a particularly fine meal while normal conversation began again, although several heads were turned to examine their extraordinary fellow resident who had just returned from an equally extraordinary journey.

When the meal ended and grace had been said, Mother Angelica clapped her hands sharply to get the men's attention.

"Now, Your Eminence, I shall, officially welcome you back. You have nearly sent all of us to jail for what you did to our town; you have turned us upside down in our efforts to fix what you had done. *However*, I have to admit I'm very glad you are back home where you belong, and all the Sisters and the Residents feel the same.

"Yes, you are a dreadful nuisance, but you have been good for us and, as you've been hobnobbing with the great and famous in the land, you'll most probably find us fairly boring now you're back here again. So, in case you are bored, we have bought you a present" She turned to Sister Veronica, "bring it in, Sister."

Sisters Veronica and Paul were struggling to hold a large brown cardboard box which seemed to be moving. They placed it at Charles' feet.

"Open it, Eminence," commanded Angelica. Charles did so, and out jumped a large, ungainly, young pup – half, wolf-hound, half St Bernard, who took one look at Charles and leapt into his arms nearly knocking him to the floor. Once secure in Charles' arms, it began to lick his face and neck and the elderly man was struggling with the surprise – also, with the strength and weight of this pup!

He went to speak, but Angelica got in first. "Yes, it's yours, Eminence…it is your own dog. It's male, but it will have no progeny – I've seen to that – and it has a name: I've called it 'Genghis.'"

Charles was totally overcome. He cuddled the pup to his breast and kept repeating, 'Genghis, Genghis, Genghis!' As quickly as he could do so, carrying Genghis, he hurried to his room, released the dog which promptly made itself comfortable on his bed, and the old man burst into tears of joy.

The Sisters had obviously forgiven him for what he had done to their property; all the trouble he had made for them, and for the other residents. And, he now had a dog! He sat on the bed and taking the dog's head in his arms spoke to it seriously.

"Genghis, you have a terrible history behind your name. You and I are going to correct that. You are going to be the best trained dog they've ever seen, and you'll obey every single command Angelica and I give you. Is that understood?" The dog was listening intently. Charles stood up.

"Well, if it is understood, stop chewing on that pretty cushion the Sisters have especially made for us, instantly!"

* * *

The Mother Superior had a brief meeting with her community after lunch.

"Sisters, well the first hurdle is over, now be on your guard. We cannot afford another episode that effects the people of this area or we're finished." Angelica rubbed her eyes briefly.

"I'm hoping that the new dog to train will keep him occupied; but keep alert, keep your eyes open, be as suspicious as you like. However, ... just in case His Eminence might really have reformed, we'll give him the benefit of the doubt for the time being." She stood up. "It's really up to St. Francis now. We've done all we could."

The next day, Angelica went to see Charles, in his room but then found him outside, where he was training his dog Genghis. The dog wagged his tail excitedly when he saw the Sister, but remained in his sitting position, when Charles demanded it. Angelica was impressed and made that known to the Cardinal.

They chattered a few moments and then Angelica said: "Eminence, let's walk along here a little way I want to talk to you." Charles was immediately alarmed. He went to speak. Angelica shushed him with her hand.

"Eminence, I want to ask you to do something for us." Charles nodded, dreading what was to come. "I want you to address the whole crowd this morning, or this afternoon, and tell us all about your past exciting few months; the men are eaten alive by curiosity and I must admit I, personally, and all the Sisters would like to know just how you ended up Chinese, travelled to all those countries, meeting Royalty and the Prime Minister of England ... and all the rest." She rested her hand on the old man's arm.

"Eminence, are you up to doing what I ask? If you just want to wait a few weeks until you've settled down again, that's fine, but just tell me and I'll arrange it whichever way you want. I had intended waiting for a couple of weeks, but when I heard the welcome you received when you entered the dining room yesterday, I realised how the residents care for you and how interested they are in all your doings."

Charles was touched. "That's damned – I mean, very – decent of you Mother Angelica. Yes, I would like to get it over and done with. At times it was exciting, other times terrifying, and most of all completely mystifying." He cleared his throat.

"I'd be very glad to have it all behind me. I know I've caused a big number of people real grief. What I've done to Sammy will haunt me to my grave, and to all the good men here, many of whom have actually been under my care – as priests of the Archdiocese - for many years.

"I would be happy to get it all behind me and not have to go around with the Press writing things about me; making up untrue stories and generally making my life a misery. I'm secretly terrified they'll come here which means I would have to leave; I couldn't let all of you in for what I've experienced from the dratted Press."

Angelica was convinced that Charles was actually speaking the truth, and quickly arranged a time to speak when the men usually had their morning tea. He nodded and said that would be fine.

Angelica and Charles then went their separate ways with the dog walking obediently by the side of his master. When the cardinal arrived at his room he went to his desk and began to make notes, while Genghis used this time to demolish one of Angelica's sandals which he had pinched from their changing room near the kitchen.

* * *

Morning tea had just been served when Charles appeared in the community room.

He went to a lectern there and Genghis sat by his master with a strap of leather hanging from his mouth. Angelica gasped, when she recognized what was left of her sandal, but held her peace. She'd deal with that later.

Charles, who had spoken in public for decades, found himself, shy and nervous. He looked at the large group of nearly all the Sisters and the priest residents.

"Mother Angelica, all the Sisters, and my very best friends. For the first time in fifty years or more, I'm unsure of myself. Let me say that most of what happened to me was bewildering and, at times, terrifying. Let me try to start at the beginning...........

"It all began with an idea I had ...."

Mother Angelica quietly reached down and turned on the recorder she had brought with her, hidden by the skirts of her ankle-length habit. The Sisters who had to work in the kitchen would enjoy listening to this when lunch was over.

Once started Charles was fine and covered the main story in about an hour. In fact, it was close to lunchtime when he stopped. Mother Angelica immediately stood up. "Thank you, Eminence.

We could, perhaps, have a question and answer session during afternoon tea then?" Charles nodded.

"Well, get your questions ready, gentlemen, and we'll hear all the answers this afternoon." She turned to the cardinal. "Thank you, Eminence, for an interesting and cohesive account of your incredible activities. I can certainly understand why the Press would have been interested...Now, gentlemen, lunch is almost upon us, so off you go and freshen yourselves up. Thank you, gentlemen." So, saying, she turned off the recorder.

As she walked to the kitchen Angelica knew that extraordinary account *must* be true, but it sounded like an excursion into wonderland. It was difficult for her to believe such a tale; she had been working with elderly men for a long time now. However, weird as all this one was, it must be true this time.

The afternoon session went well; the questions intelligent, and, as Charles had anticipated, sometimes very difficult. They all wanted to know about the Prime Minister, the attitude of Dr Wangchi and his parents to Charles stealing his identity, and the Sisters, particularly, wanted to know all about the visit to the Palace. They began to laugh helplessly as Charles described his skating 'lesson' to the queen, her private Lady in Waiting, and her husband, the Duke.

Charles had always been a storyteller, so told the story well and often the room was filled with laughter. When he had finished, he begged the men not to ask him again about any of the things he had mentioned as he just wanted to settled back and relax at his home and theirs.

The men agreed and clapped him loudly.

The ordeal was over.

ANGELICA BEGINS A NEW AGENDA

Mother Angelica was talking on the phone to the Archbishop Samuel Spotels.

"So, you see, Your Grace, His Eminence has told us everything about it all. I hope, with all my heart that that's the end of it…What's that? …No, I think he really means it this time…Yes, I know, but perhaps he *does* really mean it…

"Yes, I agree, what a story! It's unbelievable that's he still alive…What? Yes, you're right. You and I couldn't believe he was dead, and we were proven right. I must mention that to the community! They'll laugh at me!

"No, he is keeping very quiet and as taken Genghis – yes, I know, a terrible name to give a dog…well, Attila the dear faithful old dog died, Your Grace, and we needed another dog, so it gave me a chance to do two things at once: give a gift to welcome His Eminence back, and to provide a dog, as a guard dog, for all of us. And, Your Grace – just between the two of us – it gives the Sisters something to spoil, as they did our beloved Gertrude – thinking I was not aware of all they were up to!

"What was that? Well, we're thinking of going on some really unusual outings. You know, places where the bishops and priests possibly have never been before. …What kind of things? Well, I'm not sure, at the moment, but we're looking at Fun Fairs with slippery dips and carousels, or, perhaps, tours of historic villages, where they have re-enactments, or big working factories – perhaps where there are blast furnaces, and things…I want to introduce real masculine things; the men would enjoy that...

"No, I understand, I can't answer that, Your Grace. I've never been to such places either; I'll try to get information on all these suggestions. I'm inclined to the historic villages myself – you know where you can see a blacksmith at work, or sheep being shorn, or where there are baby animals and, perhaps re-enactments of various things in our history: such as 'Ned Kelly's last stand' or something like that ... What's that?" She then started to laugh...

"No, Your Grace, I'll make sure he's not the one who plays 'Ned Kelly'; we've had enough of one dead cardinal, we wouldn't survive two. I'll let you know what ideas we come up with, Your Grace….

"Sorry…Excuse me, Your Grace, I have to go; some emergency in the kitchen. God bless you ...Yes, Sister, I'm coming."

* * *

During the next week Angelica was very busy. Since the Sisters had come to the big property, the St Vincent de Paul Society had been of great assistance, as the members helped the Sisters and priests, to settle in.

Angelica was able to call upon both men and women of the Society whenever she had a real need, and they always rose to the occasion. She decided to phone the President of the local branch, Jim Fitzpatrick, and asked the help of the members in exploring the list of places she wished to be able to take the residents, on their outings. As she said to the sensible president, a good and solid family man: 'there are only so many times a man can go and look at a park!'

The president was intrigued at the task, and as most of the members of the Society were retired, they were only too happy to visit the places Angelica listed. They were to go with a definite mission: they were to see whether, in their opinion, the elderly priests would be capable of such visits; whether they were too dangerous to consider, or were not challenging enough, to arouse their curiosity and their interest.

After one week, Angelica had a list of destinations that could be possible. She called a meeting of the residents and told them of her plan. She listed the places that had been thought – by the SVDP – to be suitable for them.

The residents were asked to vote on the ones they most wanted to see first. Charles immediately took charge of the election and soon all the men were writing furiously.

Mother Angelica was not really surprised to find that the visit to the Historic Village came first on the list of preferences, followed by a visit to the Horse Races and coming in third, the blast furnaces an equal tie with a Football match.

Angelica could not say so, but she smiled as she read the results; she thought they were the exact ones she would have chosen herself, had she been able to do so. She announced that, if all the arrangements could be made, they would make the outing for the following Saturday, as on that day, it was listed, in the brochure she had read, there would be a re-enactment after the lunch break.

They would make it a long excursion and would be away for, hopefully, three hours altogether, perhaps more.

She was immediately asked about toilet facilities. Angelica promised she would find out all the necessary information before the final decision was made.

The meeting broke up amid a burst of excited chattering from the men.

***

Angelica left the meeting and phoned Mrs Maureen Fitzpatrick, the wife of Jim, the President, of the local St Vincent de Paul Society.

"Maureen? It's Mother Angelica here. Your good husband told me you went with him to the Historic Village? …Yes, that's right. We hope to go next Saturday if I can get a booking with the larger bus. I'll take five Sisters with me, four are RNs – just in case we have any trouble.

"Maureen, I need some personal information, re toilets. I couldn't bring myself to ask your husband about these. Would you tell me what they have at the Village? …Oh, *two* Disabled Toilets? …That's wonderful! What about separate Men and Women's toilets? …Yes? This is sounding better by the minute; so, there's plenty of toilets.

"What about getting about? Any drays, or carts, or anything that would help the more fragile residents to enjoy the day? … Oh, that's good! A Train? …What? …Also, a horse and dray? That's wonderful! And Maureen," Angelica lowered her voice, "Is there a small historic house, or shed, where the Sisters could use to eat their sandwiches privately? …Great, then, I think we're in business. Thanks for everything, Maureen and God bless."

Angelica was about to leave the room, when she remembered she had not asked about costs. Drat! Well, if they allowed, perhaps $20 for each resident, that should be enough.

She knew that some of the residents were well off, but the others had only the Aged Pension and most of that went to pay for their food and lodging, as per the Government ruling.

Angelica was perturbed about this for a few minutes, then reproved herself. 'Phone the place you stupid woman' she said to herself, and looking up the number, was soon in conversation with the Manager.

He assured her that $20, for each person, would cover all the costs; he'd give them a special concession, as he did to all Aged Care Facilities, and there would be a substantial discount of the entry and all other costs. He'd personally arrange it.

Angelica was delighted; it all now seemed possible, not a pie in the sky. If there was any shortfall, she decided, the Sisters would pick up the tab: no one who didn't have the money would miss out on anything, while she was in charge.

PRELUDE TO FIRST MOVEMENT

Now that the outing had been officially announced, Charles felt free to act.

He gathered his cronies together: Belcher, Stinko, and Ted. He had them all studying the web page of the Historic Village chosen and they were impressed. They read, with delight, on their special 're-enactment' days, a mob riot, as extras, posing as Irish convicts, re-created the Battle of Vinegar Hill and were mercilessly mowed down by the Government Military soldiers and guards. The visitors were encouraged to participate in the re-enactment – either as convicts or guards.

The men whistled in their delight. They would certainly 'participate' with a will! Reading on, they found that guns and bullets would be handed out for the men and women who wanted to be involved. The St John's Ambulance cadets would be involved to attend to the 'pretend' injured.

The little group found that, as Angelica had said, next Saturday was one of the days in which the re-enactment would take place. Charles now understood this was the reason Angelica had chosen that particular day for the outing; therefore, she must be in favour of them participating, so he felt free to act.

That night Charles rang Archbishop Samuel Spotels.

"I don't wish to complain, Your Grace, but it has been weeks since you came out to see me…us…*the Sisters*, I mean…What? You've been busy? Doing what? …You know well, that job is a breeze for any bright fellow…No, I said any *bright* fellow….Yes, well, six official functions in one week is a bit of an ordeal, but think of all the lovely food you get to eat…What? …Nonsense! You can't eat at these functions? …Look, offer it up for poor, starving people…

"This must be a bad line; I thought I heard a raspberry…Oh, it *was* you? All right, all right! I'll stop.

"Listen, Sammy, I truly miss you; that's the gist of the matter. Can't you and your 'side-kicks' get a day off and come out to the sticks to see us? All the men want to see you and I want you to meet my new dog … Ah! I thought that would interest you. His name is 'Genghis' … yes, well Mother Angelica named him…

"No, he's gentle as a lamb, but I think he'd tear a burglar to pieces; he's very big and strong, but he's also as gentle as a lamb… What? …Well, he's supposed to sleep in his own little kennel near the back door, but…just between you and me… he sleeps, either on, or under, my bed most nights…Yes, well, I make sure I've got him out before the Sisters see him…His breed? …Well, let's say, he's a 'Bitsa' – a bit of this and a bit of that!

"However, his breed doesn't matter, he's a very big, intelligent and loving dog who thinks his whole job in this place is to keep us all safe, so that's good, isn't it?

"Good! then you'll come out soon? No, *not* next Saturday; we're going to an Historic Village and going to participate in dray rides, and a blacksmith's work and check out the baby animals and have a *quiet* day reviving the past…What? Another vulgar raspberry! Now, listen here, you young whippersnapper, you're going too far…All right! …All right! I won't say it then.

"OK, son, I do realise how busy you are, and all the engagements you have to keep, but when you can, don't forget us. Bring Jack Okiama and Izzy Grim out to see us when you can...God bless, son; pray for this old sinner, won't you."

As Charles put down his phone, he realised he had called the Archbishop 'son'.

Well, I couldn't help it, he thought to himself; that's what I've always thought of him as... a son. God keep the young bloke safe in the dangerous world he now lives in.

Charles went to the chapel to pray for his protégé.

SAMMY PLANS ESCAPE MEASURES

Back at Bishop House, Sammy sat still after the cardinal's call. He realised, with a guilty sensation, it *had* been months since Charles had been home from his travels, and he had not visited them once in all that time.

It was not only Charles that he had overlooked, but those good Sisters who had the onerous job of facing those residents - most of them villains - everyday. He should have made time to get out there. He buzzed for his VG and asked his secretary to stop work for a few minutes.

When Fr Jack Okiama arrived in the office, he found a cup waiting for him, with Monsignor Grim and the archbishop, already drinking their coffee.

"Sit down Jack," invited the Archbishop. "I need your help." Fr Okiama quickly made his coffee and joined the two men in the big chairs next to the official desk.

"I want to talk about a visit to His Eminence...Stop grinning Jack! Yes, I know he's one of the greatest villains in the whole bunch, but he also is a very great man and we're neglecting him, and all the other old priests, out at St Francis Home." Sammy paused and looked steadily at his two closest assistants – and friends - the only ones who ever saw the Archbishop as he really was.

"I'm aware," he went on, "of one of the greatest dangers of this job, and that is, that it can overwhelm you. Both of you, and I, have to face problems and commitments day and night, which very few other priests have to face; we attend so many meetings we go dizzy; we prepare talks and sermons and have so many ceremonial duties, and 'Openings' and 'Closings' and attend more funerals, than just about every other priest is ever asked to do." Sammy paused for breath.

"Now, we need to have a break, or we'll go nuts. I suggest we take up some Sport – doesn't matter what it is as long as it gets us out at least one night a week, for practice, or training. I've often thought we should change the name of this building from 'Bishop House' to 'Stalag 17' – the famous, or infamous, WW2 German Prison of War Camp.

"Or, if Sport doesn't appeal to you, what about some hobby that you've always wanted to pursue – doesn't matter how silly it sounds." Sammy looked with affection at his secretary, the ever-reliable Monsignor Isidore Grim.

"Let's start with you, Izzy. In your secret heart what have you always wanted to pursue, but didn't have the time before? The truth now!"

The Monsignor flushed. "Well, Your Grace, as you've demanded we tell the truth, I have to admit that I've always wanted to learn Archery." He laughed, naturally. "I think it's due to all the Robin Hood stories I read as a kid."

The Archbishop smiled. "Well, it's a very wonderful Sport and I, too, would have liked to have done that. OK. Let's say that's what you're going to do for relaxation. I leave it to you to find out *where* you learn this, *how* you learn this and, especially, *WHEN* you would have to be away learning your new craft – I need to know the night, or time, each week, Izzy, so I can use a temporary secretary for that period." He now smiled at his VG.

"Right, Jack! Now it's your turn." The Vicar General blushed beetroot red. "Come on, Jack. It's only Izzy and me; no one else will know your guilty secret. It isn't Ballet, or Needlework, is it"

Jack Okiama hooted with laughter. "Not quite, but it's close. Everyone knows I'm half Japanese and half American, but my father, God rest his soul, was a wonderful man – the model of all that we could hope for in a Christian father. It was he, not my mother, who brought me to the Faith – just as Izzy's father did for him – and for that I revere him and pray for him every day. He refused to teach me Japanese, said I had to make English my first, and true language.

"As a result, I never spoke in Japanese with him in all the years we lived as a family. After he died, and I had to cope with my mother's tragic grief, she began to speak only in Japanese – she spoke it perfectly – and while she was dying, saying my father's name over and over, I wished then I had at least some words that I could have said to her, in Japanese.

"I made a secret promise to myself that, if ever I had the chance, I would learn my father's language in thanksgiving for what that great and noble man did for me." His eyes were started to glisten. "Now, I'm making an utter fool of myself, Your Grace, and I beg your pardon. This is hardly the behaviour of a VG." He blew his nose violently and gazed out the window.

Sammy swiftly came to the rescue. "Well, we can start that immediately. Jack, get onto the language colleges and see if there are night courses you could take in Japanese. I'm sure there will be some 'on-line', but I'd prefer if you see if you can attend *in person* somewhere; it's essential to get out of this building, at least once a week. I insist on that. even if it's only to go to the stupid Movies."

Jack's held up his hand again. Sammy nodded and waited for the younger man to speak.

"There's a second part of the request, Your Grace," added the VG. "Along with the spoken language I'd love to learn the Japanese art of Calligraphy. Would that be possible do you think?"

"I haven't a clue where you would learn that, but I'm familiar with Japanese Calligraphy; it's stunningly beautiful. Boy! If you master that, lad, then you'll have to promise you'll teach Izzy and me to do it as well. What do you say Izzy?"

"I can't promise to be able to do it, ever," laughed the secretary, "but I'd *love* to try to be able to do it." He turned to the VG. "Jack, I'd also love to learn Japanese as well, so as we live in the same unit, it would help both of us if we learned the language together; we could then talk in Japanese and the Boss, here, wouldn't know what we were saying about him."

Sammy laughed with real delight. As far as he could remember, that was the first time Izzy had actually made a joke, in front of him. Thank God for that, and thank God, he thought, for giving me these great men to work with.

He knocked his knuckles on the coffee table. "Now, back to business chaps. Izzy," he turned to the secretary. "See if you can cook the books and try to arrange that we are free next Monday. If you can, we'll take off and visit the Retirement Home. Let me know as soon as you manage to arrange it; then phone Mother Angelica and let her know.

"Make sure you let Mother know this is a '*day-off visit*', so no big preparations, a simple Mass, no events organized just for us. Tell her it's a *day out for us*, so the least amount of ceremonial as possible. She'll understand; she's a very sensible, intelligent woman."

The archbishop stood up. The men knew the little interlude was over.

Sammy spoke crisply. "Izzy, keep me informed re the Archery; I'll be very interested in your hobby; Jack, let me know about the Japanese language, and how you and Izzy are getting on with it; I also want to know your progress with the calligraphy. If you're any good, we might use your work on our official Christmas Cards this year." Sammy moved back behind his desk.

"Get me those statistics again, please Izzy. I must get them into my thick head before the meeting tonight."

They were back at work again.

BEING YOUNG AND IN LOVE: A POTENTIALLY DEADLY COMBINATION

Nat Jeffreys was a troubled young man. As with any young man it was about a woman. But not just any woman, it was about the beautiful Dianne Rowley.

Nat couldn't believe his luck that the most beautiful girl in his neighbourhood would even be interested in him. He wasn't much to look at; his family wasn't wealthy, and he had a pretty ridiculous job: living dressing and acting, as if he were living in 1804, not in the modern world of the 21st century.

Dianne, however, had been interested, and more than interested; she had agreed to marry him when he, after two whiskeys, summonsed up the courage to ask her to be his wife. When she said 'yes', he was walking on air. She graciously agreed to going with him to select the diamond engagement ring – which she insisted should be a large size, to show her friends – this coming Saturday.

It was this announcement that nearly demolished Nat's hopes and dreams, for he had to work, *especially* this Saturday!

Dianne Rowley had been livid. She had arranged to be off

work on Saturday morning, and, for him, *now*, to tell her he had to work and was unable to take her to the jewellery shops! That was simply 'not on'!

She had shouted at him: "Don't think I'm going to be messed about by you, you creepy nothing! If you're not there waiting for me on Saturday, then the whole deal's off! Understand?" Poor Nat had tried to explain.

"But, I can't, Dianne. I was supposed to be off, but they changed the roster; I must be there to take charge of the entire re-enactment on Saturday. It's a big promotion for me…*for us*… don't you see." Then the poor young man made it worse, by saying: "For the love of Mike, be reasonable, Dianne!

She had actually screeched at him: "How dare you? I am the most reasonable girl in the entire world." She then stood up, grabbed her handbag and flounced off, saying as she left. "Don't bother phoning or texting me. I can see what the future would be like with you. It's all over buddy!" and she was gone.

Nat had been in a trance-like state of misery ever since.

He straightened up and tried to take in what his boss was saying.

His boss at the Northern Historic Park, Bart Joyce, had been haranguing Nat about the safety measures to be used, as he was packing the bullets into the safe.

Bart Joyce was a big lumbering man, with a short temper and a irritating habit of repeating himself, several times, over the same matter. For once, Nat was glad of this, as he hadn't taken in one word, Bart had said about the bullets.

"And, as I was saying, we have always to keep in hand a good number of real bullets here for the foxes, other rodents, the blasted rabbits and so on. Unfortunately, they all have to go into the same safe as the 'pretend' bullets which will only explode and splatter coloured powder on people when they hit."

Nat came attentive and asked: "But, how do you tell the difference?"

"If you'd been listening, you'd know. I've already told you three times, but I'll repeat it. Remember this, son; you're on your own on Saturday – it's my daughter's wedding day, so I won't be here! On Saturday, then, there's no one to hold your hand if things go wrong…So, pay attention kiddo…this is your big day!

"You see," Bart went on, "there's a coloured band around each bullet. One is a blue band, the other is a gold band. So, Blue is for bad and Gold is for good. Got it?"

"No!"

Bart Joyce drew a big breath, willing himself not to explode.

"Look, son." He handed Nat a dummy bullet. "Feel it!"

"Why, it's squelchy!" Nat was truly surprised. "Why is that?"

"The real bullet is hard like steel; the pretend ones are just powder encased in stiff, specially treated, heat resistant cardboard, in order to look just like the real bullets. The phoney ones need the stiff cardboard, otherwise you couldn't fire them from a gun."

"How do the pretend ones, work?"

"As soon as they hit someone, or some*thing*, they explode, and all the powder falls out. I suppose there would be a feeling like a small slap or something like that; nothing more, though."

Nat still wasn't satisfied. "But I can't see how you can tell which is which? Tell me again."

Bart Joyce was exasperated.

"God help us! You're a dumb one! The colours are quite clear; the colour is what tells you.

"The dangerous, real, bullets are the ones with *BLUE* rings around them; the pretend bullets have a *GOLD* ring around them. Just remember: *Blue for bad and Gold for good. Right?*"

He saw that Nat still seems dazed. He tried to think of some way to help the dumb young bloke. Perhaps a rhyme? He'd try it.

"Listen carefully. '*Blue is bad for your breath and will result in your death*,' and '*Gold is for wealth and you'll kill no one else*'. Got it?"

"No!"

"Well, get it, you idiot!" Bark slammed the door of the safe shut, thrust the key into Nat's hand, and stormed out of the cell door in the fake historic jail, at the Northern Historic Park.

Nat tried his hardest to remember the rhyme. With his head ringing with: '*blue is bad for your breath and will result in your death*'; '*gold is for wealth and you'll kill no one else*,' he suddenly laughed, happily. He'd mastered it! Now he had it, thank goodness! He'd be right now!

He wiped the sweat from his face, jumped into his utility and drove off to lunch at McDonald's.

After lunch, he fell to brooding over Dianne, as he was chewing a dead French Fry, in his front teeth. He became so miserable that he went to the local pub and had a beer, then a whiskey. He began to feel better and started to whistle.

As he drove back to work, he was singing: '*Gold is bad for your health and you'll just kill yourself*'; '*Blue is good for your health and you'll earn extra wealth*'. Was that right, he wondered briefly? Well, it's close enough, he decided, whistling contentedly.

Nat Jeffreys was a very pleasant young man, but unfortunately, not a very bright one.

THE SLAUGHTER OF VINEGAR HILL

On Saturday morning there was a wonderful air of excitement running through the whole Retirement Home.

This was the day of the big Adventure! Three whole hours at the Historic, Park with the added excitement of the re-enactment to come after lunch.

The priests who were judged fit enough to go on the outing, were all up early and were waiting and ready for the bus which took off at 10.00am. Six Sisters, four of them RNs, accompanied the twenty-two men, while the other Sisters remained to provide special programmes for those not able to make the journey.

Mother Angelica was slightly disturbed to see that His Eminence had brought with him, not only the hat Angelica had encouraged all of them to bring, but a parcel which she knew had arrived for him during the past week. Perhaps flags, or maybe convict caps, she hazarded a guess.

She thought she had better investigate the parcel, when one of the men became car-sick and she had to leave her seat; warn the driver to slow down, as slow as he could, for a little while, as she attended to the man.

She bit her lips; this was a bad beginning – they hadn't even arrived at the place yet.

However, the sick priest rallied quickly, apologized to Mother and the bus was able to resume its normal speed again. Angelica resumed her seat, and by that time, had completely forgotten about Charles and his parcel.

Arriving at the Northern Historic Park, both the Sisters and the residents were astonished at the crowd of people. They had never dreamed there would be so many. The driver manoeuvred the bus into the parking area, while Angelica quickly went in search of some kind of conveyance to transport the men. It looked a fair way from the parking lot to the actual buildings.

The Manager had been on the lookout for the Retirement Home people, and had a dray filled with straw sent quickly to the parking area. It was pulled by two quiet, elderly horses. The men sat all around the edges of the long dray while the Sisters walked beside the moving vehicle, their Medical bags, each having a handy shoulder strap, slung over their shoulders.

Angelica had determined that four Sisters would take four residents each, while she and Sister Margaret would only take three residents. They had a smaller number, as they each had three of the most worrying ones. Angelica made sure Charles was in her group. She asked Sister Margaret to make sure Ted – Bishop Edward Spenser – was in her group; he needed extra care as he was using a single crutch with his artificial leg.

The Sisters had arranged that they would all meet up at lunch time; Angelica said to make it just before midday. They'd meet at the main miniature train station as there seemed to be plenty of seating there.

The Manager spoke to the Sisters and gave out the special tickets while Angelica paid what was needed. With these special tickets, the residents had entry to everything on the agenda. The Manager suggested they might like to take it in turns to start at the Black Smith's forge: it was always a favourite with men, so he encouraged them to get in early.

The six groups set out in different directions and were studiously following the printed hand-out. Sister Margaret walked everywhere alongside Ted, the amputee. She was delighted to see that Ted was managing well with just the one crutch; he was walking well. She noticed that His Eminence gave some pear-shape objects to Ted and wondered what they were; she had seen him give similar objects to Bishop Fullerton as well. She smiled as she thought of the bishop's nickname, 'Belcher'. The 'pear-shaped objects' could well be, she realised, really pears; it was the season for them.

The Black Smith's Forge was an instant hit with all the residents. The Black Smith was a burly man who had a roaring furnace going, which needed hand-pumping, so he invited every man who came in to have a turn at pumping the furnace. All the residents loved this and pumped away for as long as they could; then the next one took over. The Black Smith also invited those who thought they could manage it, to 'take a hit' with the heavy hammer onto the iron resting on the anvil. The iron was blazing red when taken from the oven.

The Smith then fashioned these pieces of iron into wonderful things such as horseshoes, and even boomerangs. All the men had a hit with the hammer, but it was too heavy for them, so they laughed and gave it up.

Some residents then visited the baby animals, while others went on the train for a ride around the whole area in order to see what they would do next. There were tea rooms where 'Tea and Damper' was available. The Sisters wanted to try this but only a couple of men were interested; most of them knew what Damper was like; they thought it terrible.

The train stopped at various little 'stations' so that the visitors could get off anywhere they liked. Some went to visit the 'Cop Shop', then the Court House, where they read the copies of the original 'Wanted' posters for mainly Horse Thieves and Rustlers of Cattle. They were very interested in the 'Wanted' notices for Bush Rangers – the scourge of early Australia.

There were several, original, bark and slab-houses; these interested everyone very much. They were permitted to enter some of these small dwellings in which guards were posted everywhere to see that no damage was done to these priceless relics which had been brought to the park from all over the country. The guards had been especially trained to be able to give proper answers to all the usual questions tourists asked, courteously and politely, while keeping a sharp look-out for any vandalism or 'pocketing' of small objects, which, in their own way, were historically priceless.

By lunchtime, nearly all the Residents were tired and glad to sit down and eat their lunch. They all met up at the main train station and sat in a group there. The Sisters had brought two big hampers of sandwiches, but they had noticed that there were freshly cooked sausages on an open fire for sale, so they bought two for each of the men – and one each for themselves!

As everyone was happily chewing sandwiches and eating sausages, Angelica signalled the other Sisters and they quietly left the area and went to the little weather-board Church of the period, which had a room behind the sanctuary. The door was open, as that good woman, Mrs Maureen Fitzpatrick had promised, so they trooped in, said the Angelus, then sat at ease, and ate their lunch – including the sausages – talking non-stop on what they had seen so far. They were delighted with the success of the whole adventure.

Sister Paul voiced her delight at the behaviour of the men. "Mother, I can't believe that His Eminence has been so wonderful today. I saw him helping so many of the residents to do things they wanted to do and being careful of every one of them. He's a treasure I think – despite all the worry..."

"Please... don't, Sister Paul!" Angelica begged. "Yes, I did notice that, but...you know...with the cardinal...?" She left off and pulled a grimace which made the Sisters laugh.

The Loud-Speaker System crackled a little as it came to life. A man's voice could be heard all over the grounds. It was the Manager, Angelica realised.

'Ladies and Gentlemen, we hope you have had a happy and interesting morning, but we are now going to prepare for our famous Re-enactment of the Battle of Vinegar Hill.

'Could I please ask all those men and women, who wish to participate in the fun, to come to the Court House where the guns and bullets will be distributed to both the English defenders of the Crown, and the convict Irish Rebels in the Battle. Remember, the bullets which will be discharged from the guns are made of a specially treated, heat resistant cardboard and contain nothing but powder of various colours. Don't worry about the powder; it does not stain clothing and will brush off easily. After collecting your rifle and bullets, you will then go to the large paddock, past the railway station, to join your respective sides.

"Another reminder: Those visitors intending to join the English side are requested to go up to the ridge area where 'Major Johnson' will direct you to your places. Those joining the Irish convicts, will gather in the lower slopes of the hill, facing the ridge, the English Soldiers, and the Militia.

'Come on everyone; this is something for young and old. You can settle old scores here today, as we re-present the great Battle – the only convict Battle in our feuding, fighting history – The Battle of Vinegar Hill.'

NAT FLEES THE SCENE

Nat Jeffreys stood in front of the open safe and stared at the hundreds of bullets. Some had the blue rings, and some had gold. He went to pick one up and his face paled; at that very moment, he realised he had completely forgotten which was which.

Which were the 'safe' ones? The *Rhyme*...what the hell was it?

His mind skittered around a dozen rhymes. '*Gold is for stealth and will worsen your health*'; '*Blue is for cold and you'll never grow old*'; No, that's not right either! He tried again: '*Blue is for witches; you'll have them in stitches*'; '*Gold is used often but only in coffins.*'

Nat swore some quite original rude words; he was sweating badly. They're coming for the damn things, he thought, and I don't know which is which! He began to tremble with terror. He'd lose his job over this ...but...even worse...what would happen if people were killed? He could go to jail!

Could anyone help him? No, he knew that Bart Joyce was the only one who knew the right code! Where the hell, *was* he? He suddenly remembered. He wondered, if he drove like a maniac, he might get to the Church to intercept his boss, before the service started.

He tried to remember the details Bart had told him about the wedding; he had gone on and on about, 'his little girl getting married'. Nat had been bored to tears listening to the same drivel, again and again.

But... Bart *did* say where he was getting married...it was... it was...why, it's quite close, Nat realised with relief. It's the local Anglican Church...that's not far away...perhaps five miles...but the time...What time did the moron say it was all happening?

Poor Nat then remembered it was going to be at 1.30 pm. He looked up at the antique clock. It was 1.20 pm now. He made a quick decision. He'd go, *NOW*!

He ran from the cell, forgetting to close the safe, and ran at great speed for his utility. Jumping in, he took off at a frantic pace, ran through two red lights and arrived at the little Church with his tyres screaming.

Leaping from the vehicle, Nat rushed to the doorway, and it was there, that Nat became aware that the organ was playing what, even he, recognized as "Here Comes the Bride."

He stood in the doorway, as his boss, Bart Joyce, proudly led his daughter slowly up the aisle. How to get to him? That was the problem. Nat then noticed on the left side of the aisle, there was a front row seat left, vacant, for the father of the bride, after he had handed over the bride to her husband.

Nat slipped quickly up the aisle and sitting in the father's seat was only inches away from his boss, who was totally unaware of his presence. Nat knew he had to get Bart's attention, and get it quickly!

Clenching his teeth together he began to hiss.

"Hisssssssst! Hissssst! ..." His 'hissing' was drowned out by the Minister, who using his big voice solemnly demanded: "Who is giving this woman to this man?"

At that very moment, Bart turned to the 'hissing' sound, and said, loudly: "What the hell do you think you're up to?" The minister thought he was being ridiculed.

"How *dare* you, Sir!"

Bart swung back to the minister: "Sorry, sir, I didn't mean you; excuse me a moment." He turned back to Nat. "What are you doing here? Who's back at the Park? Who's minding the shop?"

Nat whispered frantically. "I've forgotten the code for blue and gold. Quickly, tell me one more time. I'm sorry, I know this is wrong, but I *MUST* know."

"You, drivelling idiot!" Bart shouted. Again, the minister thought he was being addressed.

"I'll not put up with this! Wardens! Get the police. I want this rude man arrested. It's a crime to interrupt a Religious Service."

There was a long, drawn-out cry of despair from Bart's daughter, Barbara: "Daddy! *How could you*?" She then burst into tears, her bridesmaids rushing to her assistance.

Poor Bart, heard part of that: "Sir, just hold your horses for a moment, will you?" He swivelled to Nat. "Listen, I'll tell you once more, then get the hell out of here. Ok? This is it:

'*Blue is bad for your breath and will lead to your death*

Gold is good for your health and will lead to your wealth'. Now get the hell OUT!"

Bart then put his arm around his daughter. "Sorry, dear; just give me one minute more."

He leaned over, grabbed Nat by the collar, reefed him out of the pew and threw him down the aisle with such force, Nat was only a few feet from the door he had first entered. Bart, standing with his daughter at the front of the church, then, turned to the altar and spoke courteously.

"Carry on, Sir; the trouble has been dealt with; we can now get on with the Service." Bart Joyce drew in a big breath and addressing the minister again, he continued:

"You were asking…?"

* * *

Driving like a mad man, Nat was back in the Park twelve minutes later. He rushed to the jail only to find that the people had helped themselves to the bullets; there were only a dozen or so left in the big drawer.

He didn't know what to do. How could he stop it now? He could run like hell to the Manager but, by that time, it could be too late. He cursed himself for his stupidity, his laziness and his crazy mooning over that wretched Dianne – she was never worth it anyway!

Slowly he gathered up his possessions, then wrote a short letter of his resignation to the Manager, giving notice that he was leaving the Park; that he would forfeit his week's wagers for leaving in lieu of notice. If there were any need to contact him, they had his home address.

He walked slowly back to his utility and wondered about a possible job in …the Northern Territory, perhaps? Or, Western Australia? They were both about 3.000 miles away; that should be enough distance to evade the flack which he knew was only a breath away. He must make sure to fill up the car for a quick getaway. He hurried his steps; he had a lot to do before he fled the wrath to come.

As he reached the car, after depositing his letter at the Manager's office, Nat heard the first of the rifle shots *and the first of the screams*. He shivered with terror and jumped into the car and took off at a great pace.

Blue and gold, blue and gold, he thought,
I'll never forget this, even when I'm old.

THE SLAUGHTER BEGINS

It was, of course, Charles, who was the first to realise that something was wrong. He hadn't used a rifle for years, so he thought he'd get a bit of practice in, before the real fun started.

As had been spelt out in the explanation in the print-out, whenever a person was shot, the bullet would splatter them with a powdery coloured dust which would make it obvious that they were wounded, if not dead. They were then to fall to the ground and lie still, while the soldier-medics, (the St John Ambulance Cadets), would come to their aid and bandage the non-existent wounds.

Charles remembered that they were assured there was nothing to worry about, with the coloured powder; it was completely harmless. So, it was all clear what was to happen. It was now time for the residents to begin their attack on the English.

Charles gave the signal to Ted and Belcher, and the three of them let off the smoke bombs, he had brought in his parcel. Soon the people in the whole area was almost choking in the dense clouds of artificial smoke. The area now definitely resembled a real battle ground.

Charles, who only had twelve bullets, was aware that he could only spare one for practice so, carefully taking aim, he pointed his rifle at a large black bird sitting atop the flagpole. He thought it looked like a large crow. He wondered if he could possibly hit it; he'd know if he did succeed as it would then show the coloured powder they'd talked about – that is, *if* he did manage to hit the bird; he was unsure if he could do so.

He took aim carefully, pressed the trigger and the shot was certainly successful, but…Wait a minute! Wait a minute! *The bird wasn't supposed to fall down!* Was it *dead*? Charles couldn't see properly, because of the smoke, so he rushed across to the flagpole and, there at his feet was a very dead bird – there was no colour anywhere!

Charles was unsure what to do! He was distracted by rowdy shouting from the 'English' soldiers, and equal, if not more, insults were being hurled by the 'Irish' crowd of rebels. The Rebels advanced with a threatening tumult towards the English lines, which were being led by the English leader, Major Johnson.

The gallant Major was directing his contingent and they were firing almost non-stop, so many of the Irish rebels were covered with coloured powder; most of whom refused to lie down and be counted as the dead or wounded.

However, the Irish, to the amazement of everybody were scoring tremendous hits; English Government soldiers were lying in heaps everywhere; their screams were piteous in the extreme – the spectators marvelled! What acting! They sounded so genuine!

The unknown 'Father Dixon', introduced by Major Johnson, began to plead for peace, reason and tolerance; he was shot about fourteen times, and – after that barrage – never rose from the ground again. The poor man, playing the priest, was – unknown to the others – now quite dead.

It was Belcher who was shot next by an Irish rebel, who accidentally turned his rifle the wrong way, and blood began to pour from the poor bishop's arm. He began to yell for Mother

Angelica, who at that moment was trying to bind up Ted's head; he had received a shot that nicked his left ear and it bled profusely and hurt like fury.

"Holy Saint Patrick!" she exclaimed. "I thought these were supposed to be harmless bullets."

Stinko, as always, threw himself whole heartedly into the 'fake' fray. He pushed his way near to the front lines and thus put himself in the way of his fellow Irish rebels 'convicts'. He received three bullets, one in each leg and one in his shoulder. He was bleeding badly.

Angelica, not knowing *how* or *what* had happened, but realised that something *had* happened – and, it had gone wrong, shouted to her Sisters and they rushed into the melee. Two of the Sisters received shots of coloured powder from the English, before the man, standing on the ridge of the hill, playing 'Major Johnson,' understood – *at last* – that some of the bullets were real. He signalled frantically to the bugler to sound the Retreat.

Johnson then, sensibly, tied a white handkerchief to his rifle and held it high in the air – the symbol of surrender.

That was just before he, too, was shot and fell to the earth, holding his left arm which was shattered.

It was chaos! Once the error became known, the people panicked and rushed, screaming, to get out of this dangerous place, trampling over other participants.

Angelica rushed to the ridge where Major Johnson had fallen and soon was kneeling on the ground trying to bind the arm tight and shouting, at the same time, for someone in authority, to call the police, the ambulances and the real medics, as quickly as they could; men and women were dying! She had to scream out her words; the noise was horrific.

The Sisters tried to round up their own residents and keep them together in one place, while three of them rushed to Angelica, to assist with the seriously wounded, and dying. There seemed to be dozens of men in a bad way – some even dead! The Sisters were in a state of shock themselves, at the carnage they were witnessing.

Charles was standing near Angelica, ready to assist her, when he saw a man who was either drunk, or simply mad, set the nun in his sights, and as he pulled the trigger, Charles hurled himself at Angelica and brought her to the ground where she landed heavily, gasping for breath.

The other Sisters, hearing the explosion, had seen Angelica fall and were terrified she had been shot; they left the ones they were treating and ran to their Superior who was now sitting up, slightly dazed, while near her was Charles lying, frighteningly still.

Angelica, pointed at the cardinal and, gasped: "See to him quickly…He saved me!"

Sirens were heard, and soon the whole place was placed under the control of the police, while ambulances began taking away the badly wounded.

Thankfully, only four residents needed hospital attention and they were poor Belcher, Stinko, the long-suffering Ted, and a badly embarrassed Charles. Belcher, thought Angelica, would be stitched up, but Stinko would be in for some weeks of pain from his three wounds. Angelica sent Ted, just in case his ear needed more treatment, than she had given him.

As for Charles, he had been shot in the gluteus maximus, fortunately he'd been standing side-on, as he was shot; he had just risen to his feet after saving Mother Angelica. The bullet had had gone straight through the muscle and exited the other side. He was bleeding badly and suffering severe shock.

He was, of course, also furious at the ridiculous situation he was now in and that his best trousers were now ruined.

Angelica, who had, naturally, to inspect the wound, had an

insane desire to laugh. She reproached herself; yes, one could see this situation as humorous but, this man was suffering a very painful wound, and he had saved her life!

The Television and Press had arrived; Charles was ready to shoot any one of them, if they took one more photo of him. He knew full well they had taken one of him while he had been having emergency treatment with Sister Angelica kneeling behind him while his trousers and undies were around his ankles.

It was tactfully suggested by the ambulance medics, that Charles lay on his stomach, during the trip to the hospital. It would be a simple operation, they assured him; he'd only need a few stitches and he'd be back home quickly. He mumbled his thanks and said some nasty things about the 'Irish rabble' who had shot him!

Those visitors who had not been injured, and who had not participated in the battle, were encouraged to leave as quickly as they could.

As the people left the grounds, they were trapped by the television crews and urged to tell their stories; it would all appear on the TV News the same night.

The poor Manager had a chaotic mess on his hands. Even when the Sisters left with their charges, nearly one hour later, the poor man was still trying to explain, what to him, was inexplicable. It was only later when he tried to find Nat Jeffreys, and found him gone, then read the letter the man had left for him, that he began to see the cause of the problem.

In all, it was terrible day for the good people working at the Historic Park. They had to face the prospect of the whole place being shut down, especially now that they learned that thirty-two men and women had been wounded by gun fire, and – to their utter bewilderment – that seven people had been killed!

CHARLES IS IN THE NEWS AGAIN

It was Saturday night with the archbishop relaxing in his office at Bishop House, sitting quietly with music playing softly as he went over his plans for the next day.

There was the sound of feet running and with a perfunctory knock the Secretary, Monsignor Isidore burst into the room.

His Grace, Samuel Spotels uttered a wail of protest.

"Oh, no! Izzy, whenever I see you running into Bishop House office with that particular look on your face, I know something terrible has happened. Quickly, out with it!"

"Well, Your Grace, it is serious. It's His Emin…."

"NO! NO, I can't bear it! He had completely reformed, he promised me after that unbelievable idiot race round the world." The archbishop took out his handkerchief and mopped his forehead. "I'm sorry, Monsignor, just tell me please…slowly… what has he done now?"

Monsignor Isidore Grim began to smile. "Your Grace, you'll find this hard to believe but, this time – *I stress this time* – it's not what *he's* done, but what's been done *to him*?"

"What do you mean? Has he had an accident?"

"In a way you could call it that. He's been shot."

"He's been... *What*?"

"He's been shot! You see, Mother Angelica had arranged an outing to a Historic Park where they had a re-enactment of the 'Battle of Vinegar Hill', in early Australia. His Eminence, and most of the other residents, joined with hordes of other people in playing the part, of either the English Government soldiers, or the Irish convicts – most of the residents, of course, joined with the Irish convicts...."

"But they weren't mad enough to use real ammunition, were they?"

"Actually, Your Grace, yes, they were! But I hasten to add that they didn't know the bullets were real; they thought they were dummies which when they hit anyone, would explode and a burst of coloured powder was supposed to come out, on the victim. There was a mistake and the dummy bullets became mixed with real bullets. Many people were killed, while many more were wounded." He coughed apologetically. "Among those wounded was His Eminence."

"Badly?"

"Well, bad enough."

"Where was he shot?"

The secretary took a newspaper from behind his back; it was the newspaper they all dreaded. "I was hoping you wouldn't see this, Your Grace. It's fairly outrageous, I think; I believe the Press have gone too far even for this paper."

Sammy Spotels, sighed, wearily. "Show it to me Izzy. It can't be any worse than what we've seen before..." Sammy gazed at the frontpage picture – his eyes huge.

"Dear God! He's been shot in the gluteus maximus! Well, I have to admit that I've often wanted to give him a good kick there...Good God! Trust him! Why couldn't he be shot in a decent area like a leg, or an arm. No, it must be somewhere that would delight the prurient press…

"HOLY HELL! Look at the headline title:

'Our Pelvic Issues Cardinal.'

"You're dead right! I'll 'pelvic issue' the insensitive brute who took this photo and wrote that headline." The archbishop closed his eyes. He remained silent for three minutes, then looking at the Monsignor he spoke with intense weariness.

"Izzy, please prepare a statement for me to make for the morning papers, regarding this matter. Stress my belief in the freedom of the Press, but insist there must be some standards of decency displayed in regard to prominent people who had given decades of service to this country etc. etc. You know the drill. Give it to me when you're finished with it, and I see if it's OK. I simply don't have the time to do it myself; I must get ready for tomorrow.

"Don't forget we have a very busy Sunday to get through, tomorrow, with the reception after the High Mass for the Annual SVDP Society, and the presentation of awards – I've prepared the sermon, but I must practise it; then, in the afternoon, I have to officiate at the taking of final Solemn Vows for that good and faithful enclosed nun, then there will be Sung Vespers back here at the Cathedral. So, there's no way I can cut any of those, but the next day we we'll definitely go to Mount St Francis, to have a little day out with the old retired priests at the Home. They could be in a state of shock after this affair."

Sammy then took up a bundle of typed papers, from his desk, and when he spoke, his voice was uncertain, and diffident.

"On another matter, Izzy. I need your honest opinion. Advise me, please Izzy. You've typed both the sermon for the Mass, then the Vows ceremony, were they all right? Do you think I could have improved them in any way?"

"You underestimate yourself, Your Grace! You worry too much. They are both excellent. I thought the Mass sermon one of your best you've written and the one for the Reception of the Solemn Vows was greater than excellent – it was *magnificent.* I don't know how you do it!" The monsignor came closer to the desk.

"Your Grace, you know whatever my failings are, and they are many, I am totally honest, and *if those sermons were not good*, I would say things such as 'Interesting,' or 'Unusual,' or 'a little Different,' – words that mean I hate it, and think it's 'pious bosh.'

"Please, let me step out of my place, for a moment, and tell you something. You will drive yourself crazy worrying about your writings; it is a gift you have, and one that every priest would long to have, but very, very few men, actually, *do* have.

"One of the things I always look for are your quotations from the Ancient Fathers of the Church. I've studied these, of course, and heard them so often, but you actually *understand* them. You can speak of sublime things in simple and homely words, whether they are originally written in Latin or Greek. That is a gift from God Himself!"

The Monsignor laughed naturally and stepped back from the desk. "Now in order to get back to our normal relationship, I can tell you, straight-out, you need to change your shampoo; you have dandruff on your shoulders and that will never do; while I've told you before that you can't wear your pyjama coat under your cassock; it sticks up at the back and God help us if some enterprising photographer happened to see that in one of your photos. You must remember that you are likely to be in the lens of a photographer at any time of the day, or night, as well......There! We're back to normal."

"Thank you, Izzy. You're worth your weight in gold.

"Listen, as a friend, not as a dogsbody in the background –

who does all the hack work – should we cancel the trip to the Home on Monday or not? I'd like to go, but Charles won't be there, I wouldn't think, nor the good bishops Spenser and Fullerton. What do you honestly think?"

Monsignor Grim didn't hesitate. "Go, Your Grace. The Sisters are expecting us, as are all the resident priests, and if His Eminence is still in hospital, we could call in there in the afternoon to see him.

"I think, after what those good nuns have been through, on their day out, we can't, *not* go!"

"OK, Izzy, that's settled then. I'm happy with your advice. Now, let me see that damn list of names I must remember when giving out the awards – I thought I had remembered them, but now I think I forgotten some." As the Secretary went to leave, Sammy added:

"I'll phone Mother Angelica and tell her the trip's still on."

THE PRESS; THE FOURTH ESTATE

The men at Bishop House tried to pretend the Sunday papers were not there. All three of them were so busy that it was not until evening, when the day's work was over, that they had leisure to sit and read what the Press had to say about the disastrous outing to the Historic Village.

The three priests were dreading opening one particular newspaper, well known for its scandalous, and scurrilous, reporting of the news. Its headlines screamed:

'THE BATTL OF VINEGAR HILL BROUGHT TO LIFE AGAIN IN THE GOOD OLD-FASHIONED MANNER OF FISTS AND GUNS!'

There was a by-line which read:

'32 WOUNDED 7 DEAD' –
A HAPPY DAY OUT FOR ALL THE FAMILY!'

One particular headline irritated the men greatly:

'PRIESTS, OLD AND YOUNG, REVEAL WHAT THEY HAVE UNDER THEIR CASSOCKS
THE BARE FACTS REVEALED!' (See photos page three.)'

"The filthy bastards," commented Jack Okiama loudly only to blush red the next minute at what he had said. He went to apologize to the archbishop, who waved his hand dismissing the remark.

"Look, Your Grace," continued Jack, "that good nun Mother Angelica is kneeling behind His Eminence, treating him, possibly trying to stop the bleeding, and she is made to look like a trollop!"

Izzy seconded the remark. "Your Grace, I don't think I made the complaint strong enough. And," his voice became angrier, "I want to know why they haven't even acknowledged our comments anywhere? the rotten creeps! It took me nearly an hour to write the damn stuff!"

Sammy sighed as he skimmed through the pages. "No, Izzy, they have published it. Look at page eight, under the advertisement for Haemorrhoids…the…… No! Stop it!"

Sammy looked up at his two assistants. "Let's try to keep this in proportion. We know well what that paper is like; their love of scandal of any sort, not just about us. However, they exist, and we have to put up with them. There have been worse things in the past, and there will be worse in the future, I expect."

He sat up straight. "OK, it's over; we're not going to make ourselves sick worrying about it. The Press will have forgotten it by tomorrow. Don't let's get too upset about it all.

"The only thing that worries me is what the Mother General of those nuns, who lives at the Mother House in Rome, will think of Mother Angelica now, when she reads the Australian papers. I think we should send a letter off to her, Izzy, as soon as possible. We need to stress the fact that Angelica and the Sisters were working in, what had turned out to be, a very real, not pretend, battle-field; she had been shot several times; look at her habit; it's a mess of about six colours. Thank God, she was only hit by the dummy bullets but, *she was shot*, just as much as the cardinal was."

Sammy crossed himself quickly. "She could have been among the dead! What a dreadful, dreadful thought; the whole place up there depends upon her, and all the Sisters regard her as their most precious asset."

Monsignor Izzy Grim was vocal in his agreement. He suggested he draft a letter and they could take it with them the next day and, perhaps send it by fax, or email, to Mother General, once Angelica had seen it and approved it. The archbishop agreed with that sensible suggestion; it would be acted upon.

* * *

Monday broke with the sun promising real heat to come, and the three 'escapees' – as they named themselves, rejoiced that it was a beautiful day for their journey.

They wanted to take something to the Home but didn't know what to take. As Jack pointed out, they grew all their vegetables, they had fruit trees everywhere; they had plenty of milk on hand from their little herd of cows…what else do they need?

As they piled into the official car, the Archbishop asked his VG to sit in the front, with the Monsignor, and lead the Rosary in Japanese. By sitting in the front, the Mons would also be able to listen – as he drove – as Jack recited the long prayer.

Sammy had been delighted that his VG, Jack Okiama, had taken his suggestion very seriously; he was well immersed now in his study of his father's native language. So much so, that he could now say the Rosary in Japanese. The Monsignor and Sammy had mastered one half of the 'Hail Mary' – that was all.

Jack interrupted the prayer with a suggestion of a gift for the Home which could be a possible solution to their problem. "What about beer for the men? Of course, they have some for festive occasion and enjoy it; we know that from previous visits, so that's something we know that the men would appreciate, I think."

His two companions seconded his suggestion and kept their eyes open for a suitable place to buy alcohol where they would not be the object of great scrutiny. After yesterday's newspapers, Sammy was anxious not to give the Press any more opportunities for them to vent their spite, or to portray them as alcoholics.

They found a way-side Hotel and Jack slipped out and quickly bought a couple of dozen cans; that should do, he thought, and within ten minutes they were back on the road, with the Rosary continuing in Japanese. They were nearly at the end of the prayer when they recognized the various aspects of the area with which they had grown familiar. They had only to turn right at the next turn and they'd be there.

Monsignor turned right and jumped on the brakes, bringing the car to a screeching halt.

"What the hell!" Jack shouted, while in the back, Sammy shouted even louder: "Have you gone mad, Izzy? Have we hit something?"

Monsignor turned a pasty shade as he answered his Archbishop. "Your Grace, I think we've nearly hit a…*cow*!"

"Holy Hell! A cow?" Sammy then noticed the figures running in all directions trying to get the cows back. "Look! It's the old priests! Their cows are loose. Right! out of the car, but Izzy try to get the car to the side of the road first; we don't want a big hole in one side."

The monsignor backed and then managed to get the big car just off the road, then all three men jumped out to assist in the chaos.

The old priests had certainly come to know the cows as pets, but they had never tried to round them up before, or control them, in any way. Izzy and Jack, automatically reverted to their farm upbringing, and soon had the herd marshalled together and moving towards the big gates which they noticed were smashed on one side.

One of the old monks, who lived at the Home, ran forward and called the leading cow's name: '*MILDRED*' in a loud and authoritative voice. The lead cow looked up and seeing the old man, immediately turned back, and as soon as she did, the rest of the herd followed her back inside the gates. It was only then that Sammy saw several nuns, who had been hidden by the cows standing, looking shame-faced at their Archbishop who had been attempting to be a cow-herder. Angelica hurried forward.

"Your Grace, what a dreadful welcome! And, we were so happy to hear you were coming. We've had a little disaster. The cows were just an added complication. You see, there's been a problem…"

Sammy felt weak in his knees. He knew before the Superior spelt it out that Charles would be involved.

"Tell me quickly; what has he done? We might be able to help."

Angelica's answer surprised him. "No, Your Grace, it's not the cardinal; it's poor old Father Ken Healey. He's from the locked section…Oh, I don't think you've seen that area, Your Grace. It's for the men who have severe dementia."

"I understand; what happened?"

"Somehow or other, Father Ken Healey escaped. Someone must have forgotten to lock the door as they came out - one of the Sisters… Anyhow, Father Healey took off at the speed of light, out of the building, and shot off down the drive, after first releasing the cows.

Angelica continued, breathlessly: "Well, the cardinal rushed to chase him and bring him back."

I knew he'd be involved, muttered Sammy!

"Unfortunately, His Eminence then had the idea of taking the tractor – he was frightened to use the car, and the tractor is much easier to drive – and took off at a furious rate after Ken Healey. In his haste he knocked down one side of the gate and has gone off at a furious pace towards the creek..."

"Where's the creek?"

"It's about half a mile further down this way where the road turns sharply right, and the creek, which is very deep with swift running water, is in a direct straight line with the road. Eminence thought Healey could drown.

"Your Grace, Eminence does not know how to drive the tractor; Sister Maria is raging mad at what she sees as the destruction of HER tractor and has gone off at a frantic pace after His Eminence ...God alone knows what is happening there now." Angelica staggered a little, and Sammy reached out his arms, and held the nearly exhausted woman.

"Leave it to us, Mother. We'll get both of them, or do our very best. Just wait here." He raised his big voice. "Gentlemen, come and look after Mother Angelica, and then all go back inside your home. We will attend to it...And, men, two of you, take Mother's arms; she's had a very rough few days." He turned to his men.

"OK, fellows, let's see just how fit you both are. Right, off you go!"

The VG and the Monsignor took off at an alarming pace determining to be first at the creek. The Archbishop got back into the big car and slowly drove it as far as it was safe to do so. He then got out to see a strange sight.

HEROIC STRUGGLE AND SAMMY LOSES HIS COOL

Charles had been mangling the gears of the tractor, as he tore down the road, towards the creek, wincing at the pain in his rear.

He had only heard about the creek; he had never seen it himself. When the road suddenly turned right, he was unprepared and swerved desperately to avoid the creek, which suddenly had been straight in front of him.

He'd reefed the tractor wheel over to one side with such force, that the machine had fallen over on its side, tossing the old cardinal into the water, where a completely demented Father Ken Healey grabbed him. The old demented priest was close to drowning.

Healey was vaguely aware he was clinging to another man in something and he blamed his Presbytery housekeeper, Mrs Gainsbury for the trouble he was in. Charles went down deep and arose spluttering, now aware he had a crazy man holding his arms to his sides and making it almost impossible to save either himself, or the drowning man.

Charles was also now aware of the force of this water; he thought it would be a little creek with little movement. He now felt the powerful pull of the water as it dragged him along at an alarming pace.

He struggled to undo the arms holding him tightly and finally decided to submerge in the hope that the dunking would do it. He managed to get one arm free and received a spurt of water in the face from the demented man as he surfaced, continuing his mindless babble.

"......before Mrs Gainsbury; the bus is crowded today; I've left Prime in the shed with the car; He'll look after Terce; I told you we've finished Prime; we killed him off with marmalade, you forgot the mustard, Mrs Gainsbury; this bus has some Matins; get a large jar, don't be stingy: I won't have him missing that, the lazy chap – not you, Mrs Gainbury, don't be silly; the curate will be Boxing on Boxing day; every morning we; no, not 'mourning' *morning*; Mourning Becomes Electra, you know that, your husband's Greek; the Archbishop's a looney; lives with a cardinal who's mad: stark, raving, mad. The … that's enough water, Mrs Gainsbury, you can have psalm 135; never liked it. The whale was swallowed by the cardinal, tasted quite nice with mustard and marmalade… fishy taste. I'm seeing Dad tomorrow; I'm taking some mustard and marmalade; did I tell you that? yes, I'm seeing Dad, yesterday but not tomorrow, not tomorrow; yes, with marmalade and mustard you know. My High Mass. The incense helps...did I tell you? makes me sneeze……ugh…urgle!"

In order to shut him up, Charles deliberately dunked him again. Healey came up talking and spitting water at the same time. Charles felt himself starting to fail and made yet another heroic effort to get to the bank of the creek, but the torrent was too strong, and their clothes were dragging them along.

Charles, villain that he was, realised that this might be IT! Not just for the poor maniac he was holding up, but for himself as well. He began to pray, to really pray, and began by giving absolution to the dying man and then, he sank again; realising he had only moments to live!

* * *

Jack and Izzy reached the creek almost at the same moment and took in the situation at a glance. Jack, immediately began to strip at the speed of light: shoes, socks, cassock, shirt, trousers and stood by the side of the creek.

"Well, if there's any photographers about," he shouted, "they can now see the whole lot that we clerics hide beneath our cassocks!" Saying that, he dived perfectly into the water.

Jack was astonished at the force of the water and, although he was a strong swimmer, it needed all his strength to drag the two men to the side bank nearest the road. He clung onto a root from the bank, holding the cardinal by the collar; the other chap had his arms around Charles' neck almost strangling him.

"You Grace," Jack gasped. "Grab them; I can't hold them against the force of the water. Quick!" Sammy rushed into the water and mud at the side of the bank and dragged both men out. He then looked back for Jack. He was not to be seen!

"Izzy!" Sammy screamed. "Jack's been swept away."

"No! …Dear God!" shouted the Monsignor. He ripped his clothes off, as quickly as he could, and dived into the water. He could see no sign of Jack at all. To his horror he saw the water heading towards a huge water pipe several feet in diameter and, for a fraction of a second, he saw Jack only a few feet away from the Opening of the pipe.

He dived down deep, and under the water, the force was not so strong, and Izzy was able to get to Jack who seemed to be unconscious.

Izzy grabbed an arm and began the awful job of fighting against the force to the bank. As Jack had no clothes on, it was difficult to get a good hold of him, but with a gigantic burst of adrenaline, Izzy fought the water and dragged Jack to the shore, where the archbishop dragged him up the bank, checked for a pulse, couldn't find one, so began immediately to administer CPR. Izzy climbed out and collapsed, gasping, on the bank, totally exhausted.

Within seconds Jack started to spurt water from his mouth. Sammy turned him on his side and let the water get away. Jack opened his eyes. His lips mouthed the words: 'Izzy?" Sammy understood. "Yes, my boy, he's safe, he saved you."

Jack then mouthed, 'cardinal'. Again, Sammy understood.

"Knocked about, but still alive and kicking. Also, the other poor old man as well."

Jack was suddenly aware he was virtually naked. He blushed furiously and tried to sit up. Sammy smiled; he realised what Jack had remembered. "Well, I think I'll dress you just in your cassock in a minute. When we get to the Sisters, you can all get in the showers, then dress properly. OK?"

Jack smiled and whispered. "This could be my updated uniform." The archbishop laughed: "Not on your life, son. You'll soon be buttoned up as tight as you ever were!"

As the tractor had blocked the road, there were several people from the stranded cars who came to the help of the men. However, Sammy noticed another car pull up behind his car and three men rushed out with their cameras running. The name of their newspaper was blazoned on the door of the car. Sammy immediately was aware that was the paper which published all those shocking photos of the cardinal and Mother Angelica!

The archbishop stood up. He had had enough! He completely forgot his position and turned on the Press, outraged and dangerous.

"Have you obtained enough filthy pictures now, you moronic monsters? Make sure you have one of my Secretary who has stripped to save another man's life; also, of the first man recovering, who also saved another two men's lives. That is a cause for mirth; your chance to pour ridicule on them, is it?"

Izzy called softly: "Your Grace, be careful; Your Grace..." the Archbishop paid no heed; indeed, he hadn't even taken in what Izzy had said.

Two good men from other cars, quickly ran to help dress Jack and Izzy; they also packed the old cardinal and the manic man into the big car. After that, a group of men came to Sammy's assistance. But Sammy required no assistance. He waved them back.

He continued his attack on the reporters. Every slur, every insult, every untrue thing these men had written about him came surging through him, changing him: he turned into a fighting machine, forgetting the control of himself that he had striven for always; indeed, he forgot everything he had learned; everything – all the restraint – he had fought, so hard for, over so many years.

"You perverted, ghastly purveyors of filth who turn good into evil, evil into good. Come on and fight me like a man; go on, I dare you; you haven't the guts to stand up and fight, have you; you can just sneak up behind good, decent people, either wounded, or assisting those who are saving people's lives, to make fun of them. You are a complete waste of space...

"Oh, you would, would you? Come, on! I'll take on the three of you."

As Sammy crouched in his boxer's stance, one of the reporters – a burly, thick brute of a man, struck out and hit the archbishop hard in the eye, forcing him to retreat a little. He rallied, and as another came towards him, Sammy danced around him landing frightful jabs that soon had the second man on the ground groaning.

The first man again moved in, but Sammy was ready for him this time, and hit him a ferocious punch to the stomach; then when he folded over, hit him behind the neck, with the side of his hand; the big man fell to the ground, gasping. The third man, who, attempting to appear brave, moved out, carefully, only to meet Sammy's fist, and retreated holding his hand over a badly split and bleeding lip.

The assembled crowd shouted their approval! One jovial man was shouting the odds: 20 to one the Press; odds-on favourite, the Priest!

The three Press men hastened to get up from the ground and back in the car and took off as soon as they could. The crowd cheered its departure.

Sammy stood alone, suddenly desolate – almost in despair!

He was devastated; he suddenly realised what he had done! The scandal he had given! All the consequences of his actions flooded his mind with apprehension, horror and regret. He knew he had lost complete control of himself – that had never happened before in his priestly life.

He was terrifyingly aware he could now be charged with physical assault; if that happened, he would be 'suspended' by the Papal Nuncio. He would be sent home in disgrace. He cringed at the thought of his good parents; how could they cope with the shame? What would happen to him? He could end up in jail!

And his good companions: the best men he'd ever worked with? He had quite possibly ruined their lives. They would, most probably be removed from their positions.

Dear God! How could he have been such a fool! Such an idiot! And all for what? Simply because he couldn't control his rotten temper – that's what!

He stood, silently staring at the ground. The people from the cars were strangely quiet. They were aware of the distress of this unknown priest. They stared in wonder at his black eye and his knuckles which were bleeding.

He sighed, slowly and hopelessly. He knew he had to sort out the tractor, get the road open again, and to get his crowd back to the Retirement Home.

He forced himself to actually look at the crowd and asked them to forgive him for losing his head and doing what he had done. He then thanked the people for their help and asked their pardon for the accident with the tractor. The men and women were embarrassed by Sammy's words and there was a murmuring of support for what he had done. Two of the women who had watched the whole incident, burst into tears.

Sammy was wondering if he could ask if any of the men had a winch, when one of them came from behind his utility and carried the very thing in his hands.

"We'll use that good strong tree there; that will do for the winch. Just stand back, Gents, and let the professionals get to work." The man laughed and the archbishop, silently, thanked God for these good people coming to their aid.

With the winch, the tractor was back in a position to drive in a few minutes and Sister Maria, who had remained with her 'baby' the whole time, was invited to get in and see if she could get it going, which she did without any difficulty at all. She backed expertly, turned the machine around and set off for the Home at a good pace, to the admiration of the men and women who had gathered to see the excitement.

Sammy attempted to apologize again, but They didn't want apologies; they thought he was the one of the best priests they had ever experienced. Two of the men came forward and gave him a man's hug.

The men and women wondered just *who* this priest was; he had said 'secretary'; he must be someone important to have a secretary.

Sammy, horribly aware that they would undoubtedly find out,

very soon, WHO he was, fled to the car where the recovering men were driven by Izzy, in a very wet cassock, back to the Retirement Home.

***

Mother Angelica had been informed by Sister Maria of all that had occurred, and had the four men taken off immediately for hot showers, their cassocks taken by two Sisters who were going to sponge them down and, with an iron, would attempt to see if they could dry them, at least a little.

The manic patient was taken, gently, back into his own section. He was still muttering about 'mustard and marmalade'.

However, Angelica had not been informed, of the details, of the fight; she was astonished to see the black eye of the archbishop.

Angelica went to ask a question, but seeing the state of the men, let it be. He will tell me, if he wants to, she wisely decided. He looks very unhappy and apologetic; what on earth could he have done? She wondered.

Sammy was relieved to be able to go to the showers. He was dirty and half wet by his care of his VG. By the time they were all well on the way to normal again, it was lunch time, and the Sisters handed around the glasses of the beer which the Archbishop had brought. It was exactly the right time to do so; it lessened the tension that was obvious in the condition of their visitors.

The Archbishop was late. His knuckles were being treated by Angelica as he poured out to her what he had done. "You realise what they'll do to me now, Mother?" he asked piteously. "Once the papers are out, I'll be hearing from the Papal Nuncio in Canberra. I'll be suspended and stood down; those two wonderful men who work for me could be censored. Those rotten pictures will be posted on all their evil newspapers in either this afternoon's papers, or will make the headlines, tomorrow morning."

He looked up at the nun with his injured eye. "And, with this 'shiner' how can I pretend that no one will notice. I let my guard down; a fatal flaw in boxing. Remember that, Mother... now, whenever you're in a fight, never let your guard down; it's fatal!"

Angelica bit her lips to prevent her laughing. "I'll... I'll try to remember that ... Your Grace." Then the two of them realised how ridiculous this was to say to a nun, and both laughed, naturally, at the absurdity. Sammy felt his burden lift a little.

"I was wondering, Your Grace, if it would help if I gave an interview, on how grateful we were to you, and your companions, for saving two of our sick, elderly men – Charles and 'Marmalade and Mustard', Ken Healey? What do you think?"

Sammy smiled. "Let's see what they do to me, Mother, first. If they prosecute then, I'm in the soup – I would be put 'on leave in disgrace' and an administrator would be put in my place – and, there's no need for you to be involved with that in any way." He could see she was going to object. "Please, Mother, promise me you'll wait, until I see which way the wind is blowing."

Angelica was disappointed, but eventually nodded her agreement. "Righto, Your Grace – our very unusual Archbishop, with a black eye and bruised knuckles – I promise." She stood up and sanitized her hands at the dispenser.

"Let's go into lunch; as my dearest mother used always say to the men in my family – after they had been beaten in a fight – you'll feel better after you've eaten."

"Before we go, Mother, tell me about the casualties. I know from Sister Margaret's phone call last night that the cardinal, Bishop Fullerton and Father Weber had been shot and Bishop Spenser had part of his ear shot off. Is that right? I was very surprised to see Charles back here today."

Mother Angelica informed him now, in a whisper, that, for

His Eminence, it was only a simple cleansing and stitching of the wound; it had not penetrated deeply but had sliced across the muscle, the main concern would be to watch for any infection. He had received an injection just in case - being where the wound was – infection could easily creep into the new wound; his trousers were ruined though. She'd order another pair.

She was glad of the injection now, after bumping all around in the Tractor seat, and then with all that time in the water. One good thing, that water was crystal pure, so that should be safe.

Bishop Spenser, Sammy learned, was also back again. He had lost a small piece of his ear, but it had only required cleaning and putting a protective covering to keep it safe while it healed. Bishop Fullerton had a very bad gash to his arm, but he only needed cleaning and stitching; he's back again now – with a very sore arm but it will definitely be all right.

"The only one who is still in hospital is Father Weber. Poor man, he was badly shot with three real bullets; he'll have a fairly long stay in hospital as the wounds could possibly be very serious; particular the one in the shoulder." She sighed. "It's so unfair; he only rushed to help me, the good – truly good – man. I shall travel to the hospital to see him tomorrow."

"OK, thanks, Mother. Let's go into the dining room and see if my two boys are on the way to recovery."

* * *

This time, the Archbishop did not sit at a separate table, but sat at Charles' table with his special group of friends.

Sammy noticed that Charles, now well dressed and looking grand as usual, was sitting rather stiffly, on an air cushion.

With the meal underway, the drinks being served again, the atmosphere began to lighten, and soon, jokes were flying around and cat-calls were heard as Sammy deliberately told hilarious stories of his 'life with Charlie' – many of them made up on the spur of the moment.

It was a very happy and rewarding time and all three priests from Bishop House felt at ease, and laughed, as their archbishop told 'whoppers' about things they did in their spare time.

Then he relented and told them the truth about Monsignor's Archery lessons and the VG's determination to learn his father's language, Japanese. Sammy told the men that he, himself, was dithering between, Kick Boxing and Cake Decorating. He also told them he'd welcome suggestions.

There was raucous laughter at that! Then the suggestions came thick and fast! Sammy pretended to write them down, which caused more laughter.

After lunch all those who could walk easily, went on a tour of inspection of the place with Izzy and Jack while Sammy grabbed the chance to spend some time with the two old monks, who had remained in Australia when their order moved back overseas. The 'Abbey' which was the original name of the monastery, was now the Retired Priest's Home.

He asked them to take him to their special care: their aviary. They were thrilled to be asked, and talked away, forty to the dozen, while showing off their precious, beautiful creatures to the Archbishop.

Sammy, once again, could hardly believe the affection the birds had for their keepers; they seemed to like nothing better than to nuzzle into the monks' necks. Needless to say, the monks regarded them as precious gifts from God.

The time flew and soon it was time to drive home.

During the drive back, the men chattered about many topics; none of them spoke of what was uppermost in all their minds: the newspapers tomorrow morning, with the very real possibility of the Archbishop being 'stood down'; of being suspended by the Papal Nuncio!

***

Tuesday morning, breakfast was a silent affair, as the three priests studied the newspapers. The archbishop had said the first Mass at 6.am so came to the table a little later than his staff.

The Monsignor and the VG were silent which worried Sammy greatly. They exchanged greetings soberly and went on with their breakfasts. The VG handed his boss the particular newspaper they had all been dreading. Sammy opened the paper slowly willing himself not to become angry, or to lose control of his tongue.

He quickly turned over the cover page, with the usual sensational tripe on the front, then, page two, page three, page four... The two assistants went on silently eating their breakfast their eyes cast down.

"Where is it?" he asked, angrily, thinking the men were playing jokes on him.

"*THERE'S NOTHING; NOTHING AT ALL!*" they shouted in unison, lifting up their heads, and began laughing helplessly, with relief.

"WHAT? You're joking! There must be!" The archbishop started to breathe normally again. Were they going to get away with it? Had a miracle occurred? He then spied a small notice at the bottom of page three.

> *'We regret this section is missing from today's edition. Three of our reporters were injured in a minor car accident yesterday and are resting at home. This very popular section will be back in place tomorrow.'*

Sammy read this piece aloud to his assistants. They laughed even more. The Archbishop thanked God for this reprieve, then apologized to his men for his behaviour; for forgetting himself so completely. He had behaved like a hooligan.

Sammy was just going to elaborate, contritely, on the bad example he had given, when there was a soft knock on their dining room door. Their housekeeper, Mrs Carmody, put her head around the door. Sammy noticed that his housekeeper was carefully looking at his black eye. He knew he couldn't fool her; she had brought up five sons!

"John is back with the Diplomatic Mail bag, Your Grace. He wants to see you." She lowered his voice. "I put him in your little office; he seems worried." The woman paused in the doorway. "Your Grace, when you are finished with John, would you like to come into the kitchen? I have an ice pack you could use for that eye."

The archbishop thanked the woman; assured her he'd be grateful for the ice pack, as the eye was giving him hell; quickly had a mouthful of coffee and hurried to his office. John, a young, serious man who spoke several languages, stood until the Prelate was seated.

"Excuse me for interrupting you, Your Grace, but there are a couple of serious ones this morning, I think: two from Rome, one marked urgent and both to be kept 'in petto'." Sammy thanked his special courier and asked if he would like to join the Monsignor and the VG for breakfast. The man declined graciously and left quickly.

Sammy was aware that John had deliberately averted his eyes from his damaged, 'black eye'; he didn't know whether to laugh, or to make some comment, but had decided to do nothing: to just to pretend it wasn't there.

After John had left the room, Sammy read the 'urgent' ones quickly; his eyebrows rising and his mouth starting to gape open, as he read. He closed his eyes and stood silently as he absorbed the news.

He roused himself. He must act and act *now*! He shook himself, then rang for his secretary, Monsignor Isidore Grim, and when he appeared, he motioned for him to close the door and to sit down.

There was complete silence in the room, until Sammy waited until he could control his voice. When he spoke, he spoke solemnly with utmost seriousness.

"Izzy...No! Forgive me, please... *Monsignor*...... No! I can't do it! I simply can't go on in a formal way with you, my boy! ... It'll have to remain 'Izzy', no matter what the damn protocol is supposed to be!"

"Well, I, for one, won't be complaining about that," laughed the secretary.

"OK! 'Izzy' it is! Now, how long have we been together, lad?"

"It's exactly four years, one month and six days, three hours and eleven minutes...but who's counting?" The monsignor joked. They both laughed.

"All right, then, four years! Goodness, how quickly life passes...Well, Izzy, have you any real gripes about being here; anything you'd like to change? ...What the hell! ...What I'm trying to say is: have you been happy to be working here in this rarefied atmosphere...as it were?"

The Monsignor's face became serious. He realised he was being asked these questions for a definite reason.

"Your Grace, I think I've been happier here than in any other period of my priesthood. I never want to leave..."

"Stop, right there, Izzy! I'm also very glad that you're been happy here... but, remember Izzy, the Church is an obedience. We go where we are sent; we can ask for a decision to be re-considered, but we cannot refuse; we have sworn an oath of obedience, remember..."

"Your Grace, I do understand that. You're worrying me; are you trying to tell me something?"

"Yes, damn it! I am! ...*You are going to be made a bishop!* ... Izzy!...Izzy...No, Izzy, *please*, DON'T!"

The monsignor fell backwards onto the chair, his eyes glassy, his face grey. He was mouthing the words: "No! No! No! Noooo ..... !" He was desperately trying to hold on to reality, with the shock. He kept murmuring, "*Me*, a bishop.... *Me*?"

Sammy pushed the bell and kept his finger on it, until Jack had appeared. The VG took in the scene: the archbishop standing, distraught, with real tears in his eyes; the Monsignor gasping, mumbling in the chair...What to do? What to do?

Jack shoved the archbishop back in his chair and grabbed a bottle of whiskey from the cabinet, poured a small amount, and put it into his boss's hand. The Monsignor was starting to moan slightly and trying to raise himself to stand. Jack grabbed hold of him and shoved him back into the chair, but instead of whiskey, he gave Izzy a glass of water.

The archbishop recovered fast. He took a quick gulp of whiskey and said, shakily, to his VG:

"Father Okiama, I want you to meet your new Bishop:

His excellency, Bishop Isidore Grim DD!"

"Blimey!" Jack shouted in his delight. He shook Izzy's hand and the archbishop's as well. "If ever there was a man who deserved the honour of being a Prelate, it was Izzy" ...He went to speak further when his boss shut him up...

"And, as for you – you noisy, rough-house, Japanese speaking, endless working-warrior...believe it or not, but you are not *only* the VG of the Arch-Diocese anymore, but Rome has raised you to the rank of Monsignor, so it's now:

'*The Rev, Monsignor J. Okiama VG!*' ...

Oh! No! Not you, Jack! Don't!" he cried, as the new 'Monsignor' collapsed on the floor ... out to the world.

When both men had recovered sufficiently. Sammy rang for more coffee, and the three, very subdued men, returned to the table. After a little while, Sammy spoke seriously to his two newly promoted assistants who both appeared to be in a state of shock.

"Monsignor – I must call you that, until you're consecrated a bishop – I shall ask Rome if they will permit you to be my auxiliary Bishop in the Archdiocese – I think they'll agree – so we'll still be working together, but you will be sharing my load of work and ceremonies.

"Now, you'll need your own office, well there are plenty of spare rooms on the Chancery floor in the big building, we'll take one of them for you. And you'll need a secretary. You're not having Jack, I need him. What about that very well educated, young priest who is holding the fort for the parish of dear old Bishop Fullerton. He's the administrator there and, from the reports I get, he's doing a very good job. He's young, I know, but so were you when you were promoted. I think he's worth trying; if he's not up to it, then we search further afield. Do you know him, Izzy?"

"Believe it or not, Your Grace, Bernie O'Toole is in my Archery club. I like him; he's down to earth and I think we'd work well together."

"Fine! I'll get on to him and interview him here. If he's satisfactory to me, I'll then call you in, and officially install him in the position. We'd have to get someone to replace him in the parish. Let me know, both of you, if you are particularly impressed by experienced, older, men who have never had the opportunity to be parish priests...But, we still have to fix up your new living quarters." Sammy thought for a few moments.

"Look! I want you near me for as long as I can – unfortunately, it won't be for long – then I'll know what you're doing, and you'll be close for me to consult, when I need your help. On the second floor of this building, Bishop House, where the old cardinal lived with his secretary – me – when he was the archbishop of the city, it is all vacant. The wonderful housekeeper we have, Mrs Carmody, keeps it spotless.

"I think it would be excellent for you and your secretary; possibly, this Father Bernie O'Toole. All the IT stuff is still there. It was only when I was consecrated bishop, that I moved down here…What do you think? Would you like to live there?"

"It sounds ideal, Your Grace. In that way you'd be close if I need help, and I'm sure to need that! I'd also be close to Jack…he's a mine of information, and we've always got on well together, so I wouldn't feel so isolated."

"Let's take that as done, Izzy. During the next couple of weeks move all your stuff up there and get the rooms as you want them. Remind me to speak to the housekeeper; she might need to hire more staff. You will have to sort out your Reference books. and files, so they can be taken to the Chancery building.

"Now, I must get back to my own situation, now that I'm losing Izzy. I'll start with you Jack.

"Jack, you will remain as my VG, but I want you to stay as close to Izzy as possible for the next month – to shadow his footsteps. Izzy, you have another big job to do and that is to teach Jack all the endless duties, he, as my new secretary, will need to know. Clear? … Good!

"One more thing. Perhaps the hardest thing of all: You are absolutely bound, not to breathe one word of your promotion, or your new titles for one full month…not even to your parents or families. Is that perfectly clear? Personally, I found that the most difficult of all the things I had to do."

"I will have to tell Mrs Carmody; she has to know, but she's utterly safe as regards anything that is said from Bishop House. She will help you Izzy with the move."

The Archbishop stood up.

"All right that's enough excitement for one morning. I want both of you to get going to the Chancery and start work. I'll be there in about twenty minutes; I have to see Mrs Carmody about my eye first, but remember, Jack, *stay with Izzy; you start learning to be my secretary today!*"

* * *

The next month was a whirl of activity, interviews, chancery space rearrangements, furniture removalists at the Bishop House, the top floor transformed under Mrs Carmony's direction; study of the very involved Consecration liturgical rubrics, and all the extra correspondence between Sammy and Rome, re the new auxiliary bishop.

Jack was bewildered at the number of things he was supposed to do, and remember, as the Archbishop's secretary.

However, Jack was a diligent pupil and Izzy a great teacher, so that by the time arrived for Monsignor to go on Retreat in preparation for his consecration as bishop, Jack felt reasonably confident that he would not let the archbishop down. He was so grateful he had learned to touch type years ago; it had been a great help in all his work and would be now even more.

Sammy was so busy, getting through all his normal work besides preparing for the great event of his secretary's ceremonial consecration, that he had no time to waste making social conversations, but he had to phone Mother Angelica on one important point.

* * *

He waited impatiently for Angelica to come to the phone, but as she arrived panting Sammy guessed she had been running.

"Mother, are you all right?

"A little emergency, Your Grace, in the kitchen…But it's fine now: I'm sorry I had to keep you waiting.

"I see…Can you spend a couple of minutes with me on this problem; it concerns you…"

"What on earth has gone wrong?"

"No, nothing wrong, rather marvellous in fact. Mother I have news from Rome; I can't tell you yet all about it, except that I'll have to take Charles away for a few days; I'll need him in the cathedral; we don't have another cardinal to do the job."

"I'm beginning to have dreadful premonitions, Your Grace…" Angelica cried. Sammy laughed.

"No, it's great really. But I want to ask you, without joking now, do you think Charles would be able to sustain a ceremony lasting nearly three hours? He understands the Liturgical Ritual very well – he's always been a whiz at the ceremonies; never forgets a thing, but now he is so old, I'm always worried."

"As a fully trained RN, Your Grace, with a vast experience of elderly men, I think his mind is even sharper than it ever was. He is also very physical fit; he seems to have avoided all continence problems and I have no worries about his Prostate Gland – which is a very great blessing for men who have to be in the public eye, for very long periods."

"I understand, perfectly, Mother. Well, that's a relief. I'll have to send the VG to collect the cardinal in a couple of weeks; I'll let you know definitely the day, as soon as I can. If he needs any new clothing, could you order it now; it would at least reduce the load of work we have to do at the moment. I'll also issue the invitations to you and the Sisters, also to those men you think could cope with a long ceremony, as soon as the date can be announced… OK, Mother, I'm off. Take care of yourself. When this is over, I hope to have more time to visit up there."

"Just a minute, Your Grace…please!" cried the agitated nun.

"What is it, Mother?"

"It's about His Eminence that I was going to phone you…"

"Why?"

"Well – this takes some believing – I'm still not sure it's not some scam. However, His Eminence has received a letter inviting him to travel to baptize a first-born child of a Dr Charles Wangchi! They want an answer and they will send an employee – a 'Jake something', I think it's 'Higgs' – to Australia to travel with His Eminence, all the way back to London."

"Dear God, Mother! I forgot! I received a letter from the Papal Nuncio in London, and he mentioned something about this. I can't remember the details; this other matter came up and I forgot all about the letter from London. I must chase that up. I'll contact you as soon as the Nuncio replies to my enquiry…Mother, I simply must go. God bless and keep well." Charles cut the connection.

***

Two days before the archbishop's phone call, Angelica had faced Charles across her desk. He had just handed her a letter he had received.

Mother Angelica had slowly read the letter again, her eyes puzzled, her eyebrows climbing up to her guimpe. She looked up at the tall figure of the Cardinal standing before her.

"I don't understand. It doesn't make sense, Your Eminence." She skimmed through the letter again. "*They're actually inviting you to travel to London to baptize a baby?*"

"That's it, Mother. It's their first born; they hope to call the girl, 'Charline'."

"But, why ask *you*?" Then she had realised how *that* could be taken, so she quickly, diplomatically, had added. "I can see why they would want someone, *as important as you*, to baptize their first child, but…they're in England! And they expect you to travel all that way, just to baptize their child?"

Poor Angelica had made it worse by adding. "Aren't there any bishops, or cardinals, in England that would, 'do the job', as it were?"

"I think you have forgotten, Mother," the cardinal had added, stiffly, in his haughtiest voice, "the somewhat singular events that caused me to lose my memory of *whom*, and *what*, I am."

Angelica went to speak, but Charles had talked over her. "You were present at the account of my travels; my meeting with the famous doctor and his charming parents, also his fiancé – although she wasn't that at the time; she was his head nurse – but you could say I brought them together." He smiled, remembering. "I was a match-maker."

"I see," said Mother Angelica. "I'm sorry, Eminence, I was not doubting you, I'm just trying to see how it can be done. We'll have to contact His Grace, and I hesitate to do so, at the moment, as he's terribly busy." Angelica picked up the letter again.

"I see it has come via the Diplomatic pouch; and I note the date is set for you to leave in three weeks' time…Eminence, what does it mean that they'll be sending an escort for you, from London, who will travel back with you?"

Charlie had replied, a little impatiently. "Exactly what it says, Mother. Dr Charlie Wangchi realises that I could be a little timid at travelling on my own – not that I would be, of course." He stood up even straighter. "But Charlie and I are on such good terms, that he wants to give me the royal treatment, and, as he's fabulously wealthy, he can afford to do so. He will send his father's very loyal servant, and confidante, Jake Higgs."

"Well, that explains a lot. Eminence, I'll have to get in touch with the Archbishop and you will have to have a complete medical check-up to see if you're fit to travel that great distance; then back again. I cannot give you a written permission to travel unless I get that from the doctor…thank you, Eminence, I'll get cracking; we have little time to put of number of things in place." She had nodded, and Charles realised the meeting was over.

He bounded out of the meeting, rushing to tell the others that he was soon off to London. That'll get them talking, he thought with a grin.

* * *

With only ten days to go before the consecration Sammy phoned Mother Angelica again. This time she spoke first.

"All right, Your Grace, spill the beans! Can you tell me yet what the big secret is?

"It's wonderful news, Mother. My secretary, Monsignor Grim, whom you know very well, is being raised to the Hierarchy; he is to be a bishop. The consecration is to be done the Feast of the Holy Name of Mary at 2.00pm."

"That is the most wonderful news I could have received; we all like Monsignor Grim very much; he'll make a wonderful bishop…And, the twelfth of September! What a happy choice of a day…

"Oh dear, I just remembered. What about Charles' trip to London? He is to leave on the thirteenth of September."

"Well, that's true, Mother, he's still off to London, like Dick Whittington, to see the queen!"

Mother Angelica laughed. "Well, not quite, Your Grace, but

anything could be on the cards with his Eminence."

"Apparently, Mother, the cardinal got to know Dr Charles Wangchi and his wife, Mrs Elizabeth Wangchi, very well indeed…"

"Yes, Your Grace, the Sisters reminded me of all the details of those impossible things he did overseas."

Sammy echoed her astonishment. "The amazing thing is *they want him back*! After all the trouble he caused everyone over there. Oh well! It might use up a lot of energy and, perhaps, save us from more circus tricks here. We can but hope…Now, Mother, I have little time as I know you realise, what about medical checks and tickets etc…"

"Already done, Your Grace."

"You are an efficient lady, I think we'll employ you here… Everything else, body-wise, OK?"

"Perfectly healthy. The doctor is amazed at His Eminence."

"Good! Does Charles have to respond…No don't answer that, of course he would…"

"All done!"

"What about Tickets?"

"Sent by Diplomatic post…"

"My word, this doctor must have influence…Wait a minute! What about the Papal Nuncio here, and there? …you know, all the protocol, that we must go through. "Do I have to write anything, Mother?"

"No, wouldn't think so, Your Grace."

"No, I suppose not; he was certainly in London long enough, both before tripping around the world, and after he had recovered his memory, and had returned to London. If I remember rightly, he stayed with the Cardinal of Westminster while there, so the Hierarchy certainly would know him well..." Sammy then thought of another detail.

"Where is the Baptism taking place, Mother?"

"Westminster Cathedral."

"I should have known; they'd have the best…"

Angelica cut in quickly; she knew the archbishop had little time.

"Two things more, Your Grace. Firstly, a little bit of news. The Police Superintendent for this district contacted us about the Vinegar Hill Re-enactment fiasco..."

"Yes? Don't tell me they have actually discovered the truth of that?"

"Yes, they have. It turns out the mistake was caused by a young man named Nat Jeffreys. He was detained by the police in Darwin in the Northern Territory: he'd fled there after he'd made the terrible mistake regarding the bullets. He's in jail there while extradition papers are being prepared to bring him back to this State. It appears he'll face court on multiple charges of 'Criminal Negligence' causing death."

"Well I never!" exclaimed Sammy. "I never thought we'd ever find out the secret behind that dreadful massacre." He sighed. "Now, Mother, what's the other thing?"

"Do you want us to take His Eminence to the airport from the Bishop House?"

"No, Mother we'll see him off at the airport. Wait a minute... Charles will be here for the consecration, so will you and some of the Sisters. I'll send the VG for Charles on the fourth of September – that is, in two days' time – and we'll take him to the airport the day after the consecration." Sammy lowered his voice. "I'd like to be the one to bid him farewell; he means a great deal to me."

"And, to us, too, Your Grace. Your planning is perfect; it also saves us having to make the long trip, two days running. All right, Your Grace, I think we've covered everything. The Sisters and I are looking forward to Bishop Grim's consecration as a Bishop; we've grown very fond of him over the period we've come to know him.

"If you could twist his arm, Your Grace – in a respectful manner of course – you might ask the new Bishop if he would be the Director of our annual Retreat, which is coming up soon, before Advent

"Good night, Your Grace. I am praying for good weather for the big ceremony. Keep well; the men send all their best wishes to you…and their prayers."

* * *

The VG brought Charles to Bishop House on the third of September and the whole atmosphere of the place changed from that moment on.

The archbishop greeted the cardinal politely, but without the usual genial camaraderie of his previous welcomes; it was more like a welcome to a stranger – important, but just a stranger. He took the old man to the rooms he'd be using, and spoke to him in a sharp voice, that brooked no contradiction.

"Now, Your Eminence, you will be housed in the VIP suite; you will not leave the building without my permission. Do so, and you go straight back to the Retirement Home and you will *not* proceed to London, as planned.

"Each day, you will use our chapel for your Mass and join us in the chapel for prayers; we will eat together, but there will be no other socialization. You are here to work!

"Each day you will study the Rubrics of the Consecration of a Bishop – I'm aware that you have performed this task many times before, *but not for many years now.*

"This consecration is precious to me. Monsignor Grim is one of the holiest men I have ever met. You will treat him properly. It's is *HIS* big-day, *not yours.* You will keep in the background. Of course, I know well that, as the Consecrator, you will be the most prominent person, in terms of the Ritual, but in terms of humility, I want you to think of yourself as one of the *least* important on the Sanctuary.

"Between now, and the big day, Monsignor Grim, Monsignor Okiama, you – as the consecrator – and me, as the assisting bishop, will walk through the ceremony each, and every, day.

"The VG and I will work for three hours, from very early in the morning, to try to get through the work, while the good Chancery office personnel are ready to do more than their share to get everything perfect for the occasion. Therefore, I cannot be distracted by any nonsense from you.

"You will not be given a key to the house, so any time you need to leave it you will have to ask me for the key. I have given similar instructions to all the staff – *especially* Mrs Carmody – and including the outdoor staff.

"I want you now to see to all your special clothes; see that they are perfect, then each day I want you to clean, and tidy your room, and keep it that way. Is there anything you would like to say?"

The cardinal sniffed. "I hope you don't think this a frivolous request, after that blast; but would it be in order for me – as just a humble priest – to offer, as a gift, my own Mitre to the new bishop? It is a very beautiful one."

Sammy started to weaken, he muttered, shame-faced, "Yes," then thinking quickly, said: "No ... Thank you for the offer, Eminence, but you will need it yourself for the Consecration, and also for your own use back at the Home. But I am grateful for your offer; it was very kind…" He went to speak further, when Charles cut him off:

"Well, I'll keep the mitre, but, I'd also just like to know, when are you going to hand out the Nazi uniforms; I presume as we have now joined the Neo-Nazi movement; with you, of course, as the new Fuehrer we'd be in need of the uniforms." He turned on his heel and went into his rooms.

Sammy stood fuming! That man…that wretched man! He has put me in my place with a vengeance! he realized. His face had flushed red with embarrassment at Charles' words, while another part of his brain warned him: Don't be fooled again by this – it's one of his tricks! He always makes people think they are in the wrong, never him!

Sammy straightened up. He won't let the elderly trickster catch him again…he won't…he…won't… he…*hoped* he wouldn't!

* * *

All was in preparation when the beautiful Spring day of 12th September dawned. As there were so many Masses in the Cathedral, Jack and Sammy had tried to arrange them so that those having most work in the afternoon would have their Masses over as early as possible.

The new secretary to the Bishop-in-waiting, Father Bernie O'Toole, said the first Mass at 6.00am, then Jack – the new Monsignor Okiama – said the 7.00am, Sammy said the 9.00am, while the Dean of the Cathedral sang the High Mass at 10.30am. As the Dean, Father Glen Barry, would not be participating – except for a few minutes only – in the afternoon ceremony, Sammy gave him the most tiring of the morning Masses – the long High Mass. This would give the others a chance to have their lunch before they tackled the liturgy of the afternoon.

The wonderful old sacristan, Bill Lynch, would have all that was needed for the multitude of Masses ready for each, and every priest, as they needed them. Sammy regarded him as a treasure!

Cardinal Charles York did not have to say Mass in the morning, as he would be saying the afternoon Mass which was part of the ceremony of the consecration. Sammy informed Charles that he could seize the chance to 'sleep in' so he would be fresh and not too tired for the big ordeal.

Charles had grunted in a way that should have been a warning to Sammy but, the truth was, Sammy was beset with worries about each and every detail of the afternoon's liturgy, as he, himself, had never had to *officiate* in a Consecration before; he had been the recipient at his own consecration, but never as one of the important officials.

When the priests, including Monsignor Isidore Grim, sat down to a light lunch, the Archbishop found a note from the Cardinal telling him he was taking the opportunity to do as he was told, and having a rest until he was required at 2.00pm.

Sammy shrugged, and went on with his plan to let Izzy relax in a friendly atmosphere before he had to step into the Sanctuary and 'face the multitudes'. Sammy deliberately told funny stories of past ceremonies he had participated in and problems he had faced. There was some laughter, but it was restrained – a little forced.

Both Sammy and Jack were aware they were losing Izzy. He would still be living in the same house – for a while – but the situation would then be utterly different. Izzy would no longer be 'the Mons' or even 'Izzy', he would be 'His Excellency the Most Reverend Isidore Grim D.D'.

There were a couple of speeches. Jack attempted to say a few words and couldn't go on. Sammy quickly clapped and said it was the best and shortest speech he'd ever heard. Bernie O'Toole jumped into the breech and said he would be the first priest to take on a job, and have to be taught by his own boss, how to do it! That raised a laugh.

Sammy stood up. Izzy reached out, whispering to Sammy. "Please, Your Grace, no…"

"This will be the shortest speech, even shorter than the new Monsignor Okiama's. I just want to say, and I'll use the name we have come to know – *Izzy* – that you've been a treasure; I couldn't ever had had a better secretary to help me through those difficult first months here. I was going to say we'd miss you so much it hurts, but then I remembered! No, we won't! You always hogged the Television when your wretched team – which couldn't win a competition if it tried – was attempting the impossible task of trying to beat any other team – especially mine! That's all folks!"

Everyone present laughed naturally and Sammy quickly stood up; the meal was over. They said Grace, Sammy gave Izzy a quick hug, and told him to make himself 'beautiful', as in thirty minutes, they'd be walking onto the Sanctuary. He reminded the men not to forget to use the bathroom before they left the building; to remember the ceremony was three hours long!

* * *

All the officiating priests, bishops and the archbishop were dressed and waiting for the Consecrator, Cardinal York. Sammy was looking at his wristwatch and starting to worry. Charles should be there by now. Where in the name of …he was interrupted by his personal mobile ringing.

Sammy quickly grabbed his phone from under his robes, and, to his astonishment, it was his housekeeper, Mrs Carmody, speaking urgently and fearfully. "Your Grace, come here quickly! The old cardinal has just been brought in by the police. He climbed out the window and he's been with a 'bikie' group for hours and he's fallen from his bike…he's limping badly…"

Sammy let out a wail of anguish, then muttered quietly to the distressed woman, and disconnected.

Sammy spoke sharply in a voice that boded ill for somebody. "Jack come with me, *instantly*! …Bernie, run to the choir and tell them we are running a little late and notify the organist not to start until we send a signal. *Run*! *Now*, Bernie! Go for your life! Come on Jack!"

Holding up the skirts of their robes they took off through the back steps and actually ran down all the steps to Bishop House next door to the cathedral.

***

Sammy was confronted by a pitiful sight in the kitchen. The housekeeper in her best hat – obviously dressed for the ceremony – was trying to clean Charles up with a tea towel from the sink.

Sammy stood in front of the cardinal. Charles tried his trick of looking mournful and sorry for himself. Sammy was furious.

"You have disgraced *Me; you have disgraced perhaps the best candidate you'll ever consecrate; you have disgraced all those wonderful people waiting in the Cathedral for the ceremony. You are a disgrace to the Hierarchy…*"

"Sammy…"

"Don't you dare 'Sammy' me; you'll address me properly as 'Your Grace'. Get that through your thick skull. Now stand up."

"Your Grace, I don't think I can get through the ceremony, I feel…"

"I don't give a damn how you feel; You *will* get through the ceremony and you'll do it properly…"

"But I can't walk..."

"Tough! But you're still going to do it! So, stand up Buster! *STAND UP, I SAID*." Charles lumbered to his feet. Sammy turned to the housekeeper, standing with the tea-towel to her face. "Please Mrs Carmody, what can we use to clean up the cassock? No, that doesn't really matter; it'll be hidden by the robes… Could you just slap that towel under the hot water and scrub his face and hands? That's all we have time to do."

"Your Grace, it's very hot..."

"Doesn't matter, the hotter the better; just scrub him as I'm sure you've scrubbed your boys at some stage in their lives." Sammy watched as the good woman gave Charles' face a very rough wipe-over, then reaching into her purse she pulled out a comb. "Monsignor use this. Get that mass of untidy hair into some semblance of order." Jack did as the housekeeper ordered.

Sammy surveyed the finished product. "Well done, Jack, that's fine! It's the best we can do. Grab one arm, Jack, I'll take the other, and we're going to get back to the sacristy at the speed of light. I don't care if he can't walk fast. We'll carry him, if need be, but he is *NOT GOING TO RUIN ANOTHER SINGLE THING IN HIS LIFE!*"

The two men grabbed Charles and running, half carrying, Charles, they got him back into the sacristy, where several men, under the direction of Bill Lynch, the Sacristan, dressed Charles at the speed of light.

Jack, as MC, shoved the crozier into Charles' hand slapped the mitre on his head; sent signals to the organist and the choir, while Sammy, his heart racing, bowed to the crucifix; the trumpets sounded, the procession formed and, in order of precedence, they began the long procession down the side aisle to the front doors of the Cathedral, then up that very, very long aisle to the Sanctuary.

It was not until they were all at their positions in the Sanctuary that Sammy's heart pace, returned to normal.

Later as Sammy tried to recall the ceremony in all its detail, he couldn't do it. It was all a vague blur in his mind. There were a hundred different sounds, and images crowding his head. He was aware of the symbolism, the glorious music and the hundreds of rubrics which had to be observed, as if it were happening to someone else, not to him – as though he were watching it all in a film. He knew he participated, answered the responses, moved, genuflected, bowed, and read what was to be read and sang the responses, as they were required.

That night, when it was all over, he could hardly recall any of it at all; it was like a dream that he had actively participated in.

During the ceremony, he had been vaguely aware of the wonderful organ, the magnificent singing, the huge crowd in the cathedral, the army of servers, the invited VIPs, the Press, the hand-held cameras and Television cameras rolling, but all the these images and sounds submerged in the thrilling realization that Charles was 'back in form' – *in brilliant form!* His rich, and still beautiful, voice, had rung out as he questioned the candidate as to his orthodoxy and his union with the Holy Father, while Izzy standing there in a simple alb – without vestments – had reminded Sammy of a lamb, about to be sacrificed, standing helpless…then he remembered the whole Cathedral exploding with sound as the congregation had joined in the sung responses to the long Litany in Latin.

Sammy had been shocked back into reality briefly, as he'd heard Charles's huge voice then ringing out, as he solemnly enunciated the frightening duties and obligations of a Bishop, then he'd let himself be swept up in the wonderful Gregorian Chant which poured forth golden notes and swirled them up to the ceiling; the cardinal's voice acting as a kind of 'drone' underneath the plain chant. It was then, Sammy had been reminded of the beauty of Russian Liturgical chant with their use of the 'drone'.

Sammy and the Dean had vested the new Bishop for Mass which Charles, as Consecrator, had already begun. Fully vested, Bishop Grim's hands had been anointed with chrism, before he received the Crozier, Pectoral cross, and the episcopal ring from Charles – after they had been passed from the VG, taken by Sammy and then passed on to the Consecrator, Charles.

The new Bishop then returned to the altar and began to

concelebrate the Mass with the Cardinal. This, Sammy knew well, symbolized Izzy's new place: he was now part of the Hierarchy.

The Mass was nearly over when Bishop Grim had been ceremoniously invested with the last symbols of his authority: his Mitre and Gloves. He was then led solemnly to the Throne, then between Sammy and another bishop, Izzy had been solemnly paraded around the huge cathedral, as he blessed the congregation, with the great cathedral organ pouring out a paean of praise, with all stops out.

As Sammy had watched the final Ritual Kiss of Peace between the new Bishop and the cardinal, he knew they'd managed to get through it safely.

The ceremony was over!

Hundreds of flashlights lit up the cathedral as the Press and Congregation took this last chance to capture on film a memory of this great occasion. The Press had been very active during the ceremony, as well, and the best of all the photos would appear, not only in the newspapers in tomorrow editions, but also on Television News the same night, and then, sporadically, in Church publication for months to come.

Surreptitiously, Sammy mopped his brow which was covered with sweat. He joined the long procession back to the Sacristy, the great choir with the choristers raising their voices in the Recessional, to the very rafters, a hundred feet above them.

Sammy seemed to come to in the Sacristy. He embraced the new Bishop Grim and then the old cardinal who, now looked like death, totally exhausted. Sammy realised then, how greatly this long and difficult ceremony had been for him. Realised, and felt guilty, at his insensitivity in bawling him out beforehand.

Holding the old man in his arms, he whispered. "Eminence I've never been so proud of you in my life."

Charles, on the brink of tears at these words, whispered, "And, may God forgive me, I nearly ruined everything for you, Sammy, my dearest boy."

Sammy then congratulated Jack on a magnificent job well done. He then shook hands with all the others who had participated in the ceremony not forgetting all the servers and then hurried out to thank both choirs, the Choir Master, and the organist.

He hurried back to the Sacristy and taking Charles arm, whispered: "Now, we'll sneak off; I need the bathroom, and I'm sure you do, too." The old man nodded, and they crept away before they were caught by any more people. Charles went ahead and Sammy only stopped to meet and congratulate Izzy's parents, who were looking slightly dazed and were touching their 'little boy' to see if this majestic being in front of them, covered in magnificent robes, with Crozier, Mitre, Pectoral cross and large Episcopal ring, was actually real. Izzy had kissed his mother and father and, both he and they, were trying their hardest not to burst into tears.

Izzy knew this was just the beginning; he would be doing such ceremonies, and assisting at them, for the rest of his life. It was a glorious, and equally terrifying, thought.

Sammy's VG, Monsignor Jack Okiama, had arranged a dinner for the new Bishop at a good city hotel and had thought of everything; even the transport for Mrs and Mr Grim. They would sit at the top table with the cardinal and Sammy.

There was nearly two hours to wait before the dinner, so the guests were invited to the hotel where the dinner was to be held. This would give them a chance to recover from the long ceremony, and to give Bishop Grim a chance to recover, before he would in the limelight, once again at the dinner.

When the new bishop had thanked all those who had participated, in the long and difficult ceremony, then kissed his parents again – reminding them he would see them again in two hours

– he followed Sammy and Jack back to Bishop House. He knew Mrs Carmody would have coffee ready for them.

* * *

In the Bishop House, Sammy saw to the cardinal's needs and then advised the old man to grab this chance for a short rest on the bed. He reminded Charles he had a very long flight to face the next day, so he must take it easy. He then suggested that, if Charles would accept his advice, he should skip the dinner; he'd take an apology and Charles could get a proper rest before his flight.

Charles, for once, was sensible and, as he was, in truth, really, terribly weary; he actually admitted he was exhausted. He grabbed the chance of missing the dinner and said he would have something to eat and then go to bed.

Sammy was very relieved and arranged for a simple, but good meal to be prepared by the staff for the cardinal, and assisted the old man to get out of his robes, into pyjamas and dressing gown; then he, himself, went to the chapel to give thanks; they had survived the day! When he had finished his prayers, he joined Bishop Grim in their sitting room and they sat quietly, drinking their coffee, in quiet companionship.

Sammy was amused to see that Izzy was having difficulty remembering that he was now wearing a zuchetto – the purple skull cap of a bishop. He had attempted to scratch his head and the little cap fell off. He looked sheepishly at Sammy, and they both laughed. Sammy then assured Izzy:

"You get used to it; believe me, you get used to it!"

* * *

The next morning, long before dawn, Sammy was up after a couple of hours sleep, in order to get Charles ready for his long flight.

Charles was looking better, but still was showing signs of great fatigue. Jake Higgs, who was to accompany Charles, arrived at Bishop House exactly as he had written, at 4.30am.

Jack, who was looking fairly bedraggled, brought the big car to the door and Charles, Sammy and the escort, Jake Higgs, were driven swiftly and, for the most part, silently, to the airport. Sammy and the escort helped Charles with all the formalities, and very soon it was time for the farewells.

Jack came first genuflected to Charles, kissed the episcopal ring, then shook hands with Jake, and stood back. Charles was alone with Sammy.

Sammy, aware of just how much he would miss, and would worry, about the old man did, as he often did, lapsed into comedy.

"Now, listen to me, sonny," he spoke sharply to Charles. "Remember who you are. There'll be no late nights, no bad behaviour, no embarrassment for the Royal Family and, above all, don't forget to give my love to the corgis." Charles replied with spirit.

"Thank Heavens I'm leaving this dreadful place with dictator bishops and archbishops' tedious ceremonies. I intend to kick up my heels with you not looking over my shoulder. Why, as I told Philip and Elizabeth…" The bell rang and the light came on, as the amplified voice called passengers to London to begin boarding their plane at once.

Charles stopped at once. He immediately knelt down on the floor, before Sammy, and begged humbly for a blessing.

Sammy began to remonstrate, then…seeing the distress on the face before him, he raised his hand and blessed the kneeling man, lifted him up, and kissed him on both cheeks. He noticed the tears on Charles' face and hugged the frail old man tenderly, then let him go, standing back as Jake Higgs, the escort, led the cardinal away. Soon afterward the door was closed.

Sammy cleared his throat and spoke brusquely to his VG.

"Well, Monsignor Okiama, what's on the exciting agenda today?"

"Firstly, there's your appearance at the Breakfast Meeting of the 'Fidelity Works Fund'. They have to raise a huge sum of money for the collapse of their capital; that was after the manager shot through with most of the money. They say he's living the life of Riley in the Caribbean…."

"Lucky fellow! I wonder if he needs a live-in chaplain?"

"Your Grace! Your Grace! I'm shocked to the core!"

"You're not! Tell the truth, you were thinking the same, weren't you?"

"Not quite, Your Grace, but I'll admit the thought did, briefly, waft through my brain; I gave it up when I realised you would have followed me with a clipboard and a load of questions as to the reasons I hadn't done this or that…"

"And that reminds me, Monsignor, what did you do with that poor priest we picked up after he had been beaten up, for unpaid gambling debts, near the Betting Shop?"

"He's sleeping it off in the spare room in Izzy's suite, I think."

"What about those gangster types who were after him?"

"They've left him alone; they said to tell you, they would write it all off as a bad debt. That was after you belted hell out of them…I mean…excuse me, Your Grace, after you had a quiet, well… a… courteous conversation with the two gentlemen, pointing out their unfortunate misunderstanding.

"When they could speak again – and were able to leave Emergency – they informed me, a little fearfully, they have mended their ways…they also reminded me they had both been altar boys, way back in their childhood….Stop laughing, Your Grace, they actually *did* say that!"

"Jack, I didn't intend to hit them as hard as I did…it wasn't fair…"

"Your Grace, do you realise you began your excuse exactly in the same way the Cardinal did, every time he made a terrible mess of something…"

"What nonsense! Next thing you'll be saying is that I'm growing more like him every day…Jack," Sammy looked stricken. "All joking apart…*I think I am*! What a dreadful thought!

"Look, let's cut the damn Breakfast Meeting I'm supposed to be attending – it's not my fault they let a crook be the manager of the Fund; let them fix it!

"I'll send an excuse. You're exhausted, I'm exhausted; we haven't eaten. Let's go and see if can freshen up here and have a big, hearty breakfast before we return to the grind? What do you say?"

"I agree totally. Now, the only question is, who's paying?"

"You, of course, you must pay for the honour of giving breakfast to your pious and inspiring boss…"

"OK, then if I'm paying, it'll be an easy breakfast. A small packet of crisps and a glass of coke. How does that sound?"

"It sounds revolting! I'll pay and it will be a proper breakfast. Come on. The plane's taken off ages ago. Let's go and eat!"

An hour later, refreshed and full after a truly hearty breakfast, the two men returned to the Chancery offices and the day's work began in earnest.

It was a busy morning in the Archbishop's office, with many serious and difficult phone calls that Sammy had to deal with.

By lunchtime, he was utterly fatigued. He decided he must return to Bishop House and grab a couple of hours sleep; he wouldn't get through the rest of the day if he didn't. He had packed up his notes when Jack rushed through the door.

"Your Grace, quickly pick up the phone. It's Mother Angelica and she's crying…"

"Dear God," Sammy grabbed for the phone, "well, it can't be about Charles this time……Mother? What is the trouble? … What? …I'm sorry, I don't understand, we saw the plane take off; we were at the airport…

"I see, but I still don't understand…WHAT?" he turned to the Monsignor. "Jack, listen to this…" then spoke to Angelica: "Mother rewind it and play it for the Monsignor to hear…Thank you.|" Turning again to his VG, "Jack, one of the priests taped this from the radio…Listen!

> *'The early flight QR 379 to London is reported missing. It has lost radar contact; all attempts to renew contact have been unsuccessful; we have grave fears for the safety of the flight. It would be somewhere over the Indian Ocean; the last contact was with the Maldives and that was thirty minutes ago. No trace can be found of it since….'*

* * *

Sammy sat still. He felt a shaft of fear and dread pass through his body; he could hardly breathe; he found he was holding his episcopal cross so tightly, his fingers had turned white. He attempted to stand up…

Jack, seeing the white face of his superior, touched him lightly on the arm. "Your Grace," he whispered. "Please, just sit back down, Your Grace. You'll be right in a moment..."

"I'm sorry, Jack…No, Mother, I'm speaking to the Monsignor. Mother…please I beg of you: *STOP IT*! Last time, you and I went through hell, with grief, fear, dread and worry…this time, *WE ARE NOT GOING TO DO THAT*!

"I am NOT going to go through the same agonies I went through last time…

"No! Listen to me! *Never again*! …We suffer badly, and he turns up, good as gold, every time… No, I'll just pretend I… never heard… that announcement.

"Let's make a pact, Mother! We just carry on our duties as usual and pray for that man, who WILL BE BACK! I promise you, Mother:

HE *WILL* BE BACK!"

Will he?

Perhaps!

www.ingramcontent.com/pod-product-compliance
Lightning Source LLC
LaVergne TN
LVHW011349080426
835511LV00005B/212